mettle

BIBLE READING NOTES

TO INSPIRE COURAGE SPIRIT CHARACTER

Published 2013 by CWR, Waverley Abbey House, Waverley Lane, Farnham, Surrey GU9 8EP, England. Registered Charity No. 294387. Registered Limited Company No. 1990308.

Mettle Bible-reading notes are produced in association with British Youth for Christ. British Youth for Christ is part of Youth for Christ International, a movement of youth evangelism organisations in over 100 countries of the world. Please visit www.yfci.org for the country nearest you.

Series Editor: Simeon Whiting

Contributors: Ruth Hassall, Chris Kidd, Hannah Kidd, Liz Longden, Simeon Whiting

The notes on 'Church' were previously published in *Mettle* May–Aug 2006.

See back of book for list of National Distributors.

Concept development by YFC and CWR.
Editing, design and production by CWR.

Printed in Croatia by Zrinski.

CONTENTS

WELCOME TO mettle

COURAGE SPIRIT CHARACTER ...

CHURCH OFTEN GETS a bad press. Even some Christians moan about how boring their church is or don't bother with church at all. We're aiming to present a fairer picture of the Church in this issue of *Mettle*: the Church as a movement of God's people, united throughout the world, throughout time. The Church as God's plan for humanity; as somewhere we can all belong and become more like Jesus.

We'll also unpack three Hot Potatoes: Temptation, Apologetics and Hope. You don't need us to tell you how common temptation is. We all face it, so let's give a thought to what we can do about it. Apologetics might sound a bit uninspiring, but dig a little deeper and you'll find some really valuable stuff. Knowing what we believe and why we believe it, matters. And finally, we'll look at hope – the real hope we have in Jesus and how it can make a difference to our present and our future.

ENJOY!

The *Mettle* Team

WED 1 JAN

READ:
MATTHEW 16:15–18

KEY VERSE
V18

'... you are Peter... and upon this rock I will build my church, and all the powers of hell will not conquer it.'

THE CHURCH PT1

OVER THE NEXT few weeks we are going to be looking at what the Bible says the Church is and should be like. I should explain straightaway that there is a difference between church (the local meeting place/the people who meet there) and the Church (Christians everywhere). To help, I will use lower case 'c' for the local church and upper case 'C' for the Church, Christians everywhere.

In the reading today we can see that Jesus is telling one of His disciples, Peter (whose name means

'rock'), that the Church belongs to Jesus. He will build His Church on a strong foundation. This foundation is the people who follow God – not just Peter but anyone who believes.

Jesus tells us of the Church's need for a strong foundation of people, but He also tells us that nothing, not even death and destruction, can defeat it. In a world where we are being told that the Church is not relevant and that the Church is dying as numbers dwindle, this promise from Jesus is really important.

God wants us to know what the point of His Church is – that it is actually there as a help to us and to others. He is also telling us that by being part of the Church we belong to Him. As a body of people we belong to God and He isn't going to let that body of people be destroyed in their relationship and worship of Him.

THINK

Think about your views and feelings about the Church. Are you going to believe what the world is telling you about the Church or are you going to discover for yourself the point and purpose it has in your relationship with God?

Ask God to show you the positive side of being in a church and how it can help you in your relationship with Him. Pray that He will help you be a committed part of it.

THURS 2 JAN

READ:
ACTS 20:28–32

KEY VERSE
v28

'So guard yourselves and God's people. Feed and shepherd God's flock – his church, purchased with his own blood ...'

WOW – WHAT an awesome fact! Jesus, by dying on the cross, has enabled us to have the Church and be a part of it. Not only does the Church belong to Him, but if He hadn't died on the cross it would not exist. That is how important the Church is to Him. So, we can't ignore the warning we receive from today's reading of how we must care for it.

Verse 28 also tells us that the Church needs feeding and guiding. This gives us a further clue as to what the idea of church is. Jesus realises that we are human; that we can make mistakes and get things wrong. He sees our local churches, the places where we meet with other Christians, as places where we can receive help, guidance and teaching on who He is, what He can do for us and how we can love and serve Him in return. It is a place where we can learn what is right and how we should be living our lives for God; where we can be guided by His Spirit through the help of others.

Church leaders should also 'shepherd God's flock' – take care of church members. God's Holy Spirit has appointed them to help and lead the Church.

THINK

Do you see your local church as being somewhere that you can learn more about God and be guided in how to live as part of the whole Church? Think about your church or a church you could go to and how you could help it to be more like this – or is it already?

READ: ECCLESIASTES 4:7–12

FRI 3 JAN

KEY VERSE v12

'A person standing alone can be attacked and defeated, but two can stand back-to-back and conquer.'

A NUMBER OF people I know have questioned why the Church is important. They're quick to point out the shortcomings of the church they belong to – the poor worship band, the annoying people, the problem of having to get out of bed on a Sunday morning in the first place – and ask whether they'd be better off without it. Couldn't they just live as a Christian on their own, without needing to bother with being part of a church? This might sound like a tempting option, particularly if there are people at your church you don't get on with, or if you just want to stay in bed on Sundays. But what happens if life starts going wrong? The people I know who turned their backs on the Church, effectively turned their backs on the people who would help them when they needed it. So, the next time they had to face one of life's battles, there was no one to fight alongside them. They ended up hurt – and lost their faith.

Church might not always seem like fun, but it's vital for us to help each other through life's battles. Don't try to fight alone.

THINK

Who do you have fighting alongside you in the battles you face? How can you fight for them too? Could you help someone who may be marginalising themselves in your church?

WEEKEND

4/5 JAN

READ:
COLOSSIANS 1:15–23

KEY VERSE
v18

'Christ is also the head of the church, which is his body ... he is first in everything.'

PAUL HAS A lot to say in his letters about the Church. In particular, he gives us the image of the Church being like a body. It's all about relationship: our relationship with Jesus and with each other within the Church. This image shows that church is a two-way thing. It is never just about us.

The idea of Jesus being the Head of the Church, presented in our reading today, can be looked at in various different ways. Jesus is at the centre of all that happens among His people. We, as the rest of the Body, depend on the Head. We all know how important our heads are in making the rest of our bodies work. Without Jesus the Church won't work, therefore we need to depend on Him.

We know how closely connected all the parts of our body are and this shows that we have a close connection with Jesus as the Head. Our heads influence the rest of our being by sending messages to various places. Jesus should be influencing His Body in a similar way. We should be listening and watching for messages from Jesus to see how we should be acting as one.

The second part of verse 18 points even more strongly to the idea of Jesus having influence and a ruling power over us as we see that He is such an important part of the whole of creation and future times. We should view the Church as including every believer on earth and not just people we may see in our own church or youth group week by week. If Jesus has such an important role over the whole earth then we can see that His Church has an important part to play as well.

CHALLENGE

Reread Colossians 1:15–23. This passage speaks about Jesus' supremacy and place as number one. Is Jesus supreme in your life? What does being part of Jesus' Body, the Church, mean to you?

MON 6 JAN

READ:
1 CORINTHIANS 14:12–17

KEY VERSE
v12

'Since you are so eager to have the special abilities the Spirit gives, seek those that will strengthen the whole church.'

IN CHAPTER 12 of 1 Corinthians, Paul lists different spiritual gifts that the Holy Spirit wants to give to people in the Church. Spiritual gifts are there to help people in their worship of God and their understanding of Him. In the Corinthian church there was a lot of discussion over which gifts should be more sought after – a discussion that churches still have today.

In our reading today, Paul is trying to make people see that God will give gifts that will help individual churches and therefore the Church as a whole (v12). It may be that someone wants the gift of prophecy or speaking in tongues. These are great gifts to ask for, but are they things that everyone can benefit from? Paul goes on to say that encouraging, strengthening and comforting within the churches are just as important.

Paul says love should be our highest goal (1 Cor. 13:1–3). Sometimes we can get caught up with the desire to have spiritual gifts and lose sight of the fact that they are meant to bless the whole of our church.

PRAY

Maybe you don't see the evidence of any spiritual gifts in your church. Why not spend some time talking to God about this. If there is a gift you would like to receive, ask the Holy Spirit for it. If you have not really heard about spiritual gifts before, why not find a mature Christian and speak to them about it further?

READ: EPHESIANS 2:14–22

KEY VERSE v22

'Through him you Gentiles are also being made part of this dwelling where God lives by his Spirit.'

THE CHURCH IS for all, not just for specific people as was originally taught by some. (Note: Gentiles are people who are not Jews.)

Have you ever been included in something really special where you were chosen from a group to do something? When I performed in my Sixth Form's production of *Grease* it didn't matter that I was only in the chorus and was not playing one of the named parts. I'd still been chosen and had got into the cast instead of someone else. Friends of mine who didn't get through were gutted, yet I felt that I was special enough to be chosen to sing and dance. As nervous as I was, walking into the audition, I knew that it was the only way I could be chosen and be seen as special enough to be in the cast.

God's Church is like this – we are special and chosen and He wants us to be a part of it. However, there is one big difference – it is open to all people. There is no audition. All God asks is that people repent, believe in Him and what Jesus did by dying on the cross, and accept Him into their lives. Church is somewhere that people can be in God's presence with other Christians and learn and support each other.

PRAY

Do you accept that God has a place for you in His Church? Do you see your church as a place where you too can dwell in God's presence? Pray that God will meet with you next time you are in church.

WED 8 JAN

READ:
1 CORINTHIANS 1:10–17

KEY VERSE
v10

'... live in harmony with each other. Let there be no divisions in the church. Rather, be ... united in thought and purpose.'

OVER MY YEARS of going to church I can recall times when there have been divisions among the people there. Whether over something as small as how much to charge for the tea and coffee after the Sunday service, or what kind of songs should be sung in worship, they can all cause disagreements and hurt. Unfortunately, I know people who have left churches over these kinds of arguments. So how can we be united in our churches in thought, mind and purpose?

Churches need to seek God's will in the way they operate as it is God whom we follow and to whom the whole Church belongs. Unity is a hard thing to achieve, but everyone has a part to play. If there is something you do not agree with in your church, or something you would like to see changed that is preventing unity, you need to do something about it. It could well be that others agree but do not have the courage to do anything.

The important thing to remember is that you should act in the way that Jesus would want, and seek His will. Prayerfully bring your concerns to someone in leadership and get their opinion.

THINK

God calls us to be united so that we can all benefit from worship and teaching, but how can you help your church to become more in line with this view? Stay positive if there are divisions and keep focused on what God wants you to do.

READ: EPHESIANS 4:4–6

KEY VERSE
v4

'For there is one body and one Spirit, just as you have been called to one glorious hope for the future.'

ONE BODY, ONE Spirit and one future. That is what Jesus is offering us through the Church. An amazing unity and fellowship with others and with Him, not only for now but forever – this is something He has called us to. But don't let yourself get lost in the crowd. Jesus wants each and every one of us to take up this challenge. He doesn't just see the Church as a collective, but is aware of every single person included within it. He sees our individual efforts for unity.

Being part of one Body means that we can work together to bring about God's will. We have His Holy Spirit to help us, unite us and give us peace. What we are working towards, as the Body with the Spirit's help, is a glorious future. But what is this glorious future? It is a place where we can live with God forever – heaven. Where there won't be the hurt, pain and sin of this life and earth, but a new earth full of God's love and glory. It will be somewhere you will never get bored or have horrible things to do, but where you will do everything with joy.

PRAY

Spend some time in prayer today asking for a sense of God's Spirit in your life. Ask Him to help you see the Church the way He does. Also ask Him to help you understand the future we're headed for, and how this should affect the way you live now.

FRI 10 JAN

READ:
ROMANS 12:4–8

KEY VERSE
v5

'... so it is with Christ's body. We are many parts of one body, and we all belong to each other.'

WHEN WE LOOK at the Bible we see that we were created to be in relationship with others. The whole point of God creating us was for relationship with Himself and others. When He created us He could have made us like puppets, doing exactly what He wanted, without the ability to choose. Yet instead He created us with the freedom to do what we want and the choice to follow Him or go our own way.

We can also see that God wants us to interact with others around us. He sees that together we can support and help one another. Just as He cares for the Body, so God wants us to care for each other. In John 13:34 we read, 'Love each other. Just as I have loved you ...'. Jesus gave up so much for us through love and He asks us to love and treat others in that same way.

God wants the best for us – and we should want the best for each other. One of the functions of the Church is to bring us together to love and support each other, so that we can then fulfil what God wants us to do. Supporting and loving each other will mean that we can work for God's purposes together.

CHALLENGE

Do you see why you need other Christians to help and support you in living your life and working for God's purposes? Look for people who can help you in this way. Also look for people you can support, in turn.

READ:
JAMES 1:1–12

KEY VERSE
V12

'God blesses those who patiently endure testing and temptation. Afterward they will receive the crown of life ...'

TEMPTATION PT1

YOU ARE NOT ALONE!

I CAN BE a bit of a perfectionist. When I was at primary school, I used to take great care over any work that needed copying up in neat to go on display. If I made a mistake then I got extremely frustrated. Life can be like this. We may try really hard to live perfect lives, but we always seem to mess up. Faced with temptation, we all too often give in.

You don't have to go far into the Bible before you come across temptation with Adam and Eve in the

CONTINUED»

CONTINUED»

Garden of Eden. After that, temptation keeps on cropping up again and again. Over the next two weeks we are going to be looking at some of what the Bible has to say about temptation. We will find that many of the great men and women of God faced temptation. In fact, even Jesus Himself was tempted by the devil.

Despite the fact that temptation is seemingly unavoidable, this does not mean that we should simply accept it as part and parcel of life. God does equip us with the strength that we need to stay strong in the face of temptation and there are rich rewards and blessings promised for us if we can endure it. In a few weeks' time, in the second part of our series on temptation, prepare to arm yourself with what is needed to stay strong and resist temptation from the devil.

PRAY

Father God, we confess that we have all given in to temptation in the past. Please forgive us for the times when we have chosen to please ourselves, rather than You. Help us in our resolve to resist temptation, trusting in You and Your promises for us. Amen.

READ: GENESIS 3:1–6

KEY VERSE v6

MON 13 JAN

'The woman was convinced ... she took some of the fruit and ate it ...'

WE SAID YESTERDAY that you don't have to read very far into the Bible before you come face to face with temptation. Although being tempted by a piece of forbidden fruit may seem quite far from our own experiences of temptation, Eve's temptation in the Garden of Eden can tell us a lot about how we are often tempted.

In today's reading we see that Eve knew that eating the fruit was wrong. We can sometimes kid ourselves that giving into temptation might not be wrong – we tell ourselves 'it's not that bad', 'I've known others do worse' or 'If I want it so much it can't be bad for me' – but generally, deep down, we know what is right and wrong when faced with temptation.

The serpent tempted Eve in a number of ways, by appealing both to her physical senses (the fruit looked good and would taste good) and her personal pride (the tree would give her superior knowledge). Our own temptations usually appeal to either our physical senses or our pride, if not both.

THINK

Spend some time thinking about the ways in which you may be tempted. What are your weak spots? Do you tend to be tempted by gaining physical satisfaction or by things which make you feel more proud of yourself? Ask God that He would help you to stand firm when tempted in these areas of weakness.

TUES 14 JAN

READ:
GENESIS 3:6–13

KEY VERSE
v8

'... the man and his wife heard the LORD God walking about in the garden. So they hid from the LORD God among the trees.'

WHEN I WAS young, cameras were the old fashioned type with film. For my seventh birthday I was proud to receive my first camera. I was told never to open the back of the camera when I was in the middle of a film. However, I was curious and, yes, I was tempted. One day, I opened the back of my camera to look at the film inside. I then closed it back up and hoped that nobody would find out what I had done. After that day, my camera never worked properly again. I was too scared to tell anybody as I knew that I was wrong to go against the instructions I had been given. I knew that the camera had cost a lot of money and that I had not behaved responsibly with what was a precious gift.

In today's reading, we see how Eve responds when she has given in to temptation. Yesterday, we recognised some of the features of our own temptations in Eve. We may also recognise in her our own responses when confronted by what we have done. As I did after opening the back of my camera, we may try to hide what we've done and lie to cover it up.

CHALLENGE
Spend some time thinking about when you have given in to temptation. Are there any instances that you have been trying to hide and cover up? Confess them to God now and ask for His forgiveness.

READ: JOSHUA 7:1–21

WED 15 JAN

KEY VERSE v1

'A man named Achan had stolen some of these dedicated things, so the LORD was very angry ...'

DO YOU HAVE anything that is so special to you that you hardly ever use it? My mum has a whole collection of crockery that she has never used as she is worried about it getting broken. Perhaps she is saving it in case the Queen ever comes to visit!

The Israelites had been instructed that certain things should be 'set apart for the Lord' (Josh. 7:1). But Achan disobeyed this instruction and, as a result, caused major problems for the Israelite warriors.

Once again, in this reading, we are clear that Achan knew that what he was doing was wrong. How often do you find yourself feeling as though you have done something wrong but have no idea what? Probably not very often. We are usually very aware when we have made a mistake or a bad decision.

When we give in to temptation, there are consequences and the consequences were particularly severe for Achan. But we can take comfort that, if we repent of our sins, God will forgive us. On the cross, Jesus took the punishment that we deserve, so that we can be forgiven.

THINK

Is there anything that you think God might be asking you to set apart for Him in your own life? Perhaps some of your precious time, perhaps some of your money? What temptations might stop you from setting these things apart for Him?

THURS 16 JAN

READ:
2 SAMUEL 11:1–5

KEY VERSE
v2
'As he looked out over the city, he noticed a woman of unusual beauty taking a bath.'

THE OLD TESTAMENT is riddled with stories of people who gave in to temptation. Perhaps one of the most notable people to do this was King David. David was God's chosen and anointed leader. But even a man like David succumbed to temptation. Today and tomorrow we'll look at his story in a bit more detail.

In today's reading, David sees a beautiful woman bathing and he is filled with lust. David finds out that the woman, Bathsheba, is already married. However, even though he knows it is wrong – just like Eve with the fruit – he takes what he can't have. With no thought for the consequences, David allows his temptation to control his actions.

David was not the only person in the Bible to be turned away from God's path by the temptation that comes from lust. The Bible tells us that Solomon, (David's son) '... had 700 wives of royal birth and 300 concubines. And in fact, they did turn his heart away from the LORD.' (1 Kings 11:3). One of the worst consequences of giving in to temptation is that it draws us away from God.

THINK
In what situations do you find yourself giving in to temptation without thinking of the consequences? How could you guard yourself against temptation in these situations? Or can you avoid these situations altogether?

FRI 17 JAN

READ: 2 SAMUEL 11:6–27

KEY VERSE v15

'..."Station Uriah on the front lines where the battle is fiercest. Then pull back so that he will be killed."'

YESTERDAY WE LEARNED how David slept with another man's wife and she became pregnant. It was like a storyline from a soap opera. We may have thought yesterday that things could not have got any worse. Surely David could not stoop lower than sleeping with another man's wife?

But in today's reading, David decides to try and cover up his sin and things soon get even messier. He calls for Bathsheba's husband, Uriah, who is away fighting at war, to come back home. He hopes that Uriah will sleep with his wife and therefore, everyone will assume she is pregnant through him.

Unfortunately for David, Uriah will not sleep with his wife while his comrades are still at war, even after David gets him drunk. In desperation, David arranges for Uriah to be killed. With Uriah dead, David could then take Bathsheba as his own wife.

David went to extreme lengths to hide the fact that he had given in to temptation. But whatever we've done, we can't deceive God. As David found, a selfish choice often leads to another and another, unless we own up to what we've done, turn back to God and receive His forgiveness.

PRAY

Father God, so often we weave tangled webs through our sin. Help me to admit when I have given in to temptation, to say sorry and to turn away from this way of behaving. Amen.

WEEKEND

18/19 JAN

READ:

ACTS 5:1–11

KEY VERSE

v3

'... why have you let Satan fill your heart? You lied to the Holy Spirit, and you kept some of the money for yourself.'

OVER THE LAST couple of days we have thought about David and his temptation as a result of lust. But, of course, lust is not necessarily a problem for everyone. We all have areas in which we are weak and more prone to temptation. Today we look at a couple in the New Testament who found themselves tempted by a love of money.

I recently heard a story on the radio about a woman who, every year, bought all the Christmas presents for her brother to give to other relatives. She would do his Christmas shopping for him and then present him with a bill. She confessed, however, that the amount she charged her brother was not the actual cost of the items she purchased. In fact, she always added more to the total without telling him.

Ananias and Sapphira had sold some property. It was customary for the church community at this time to pool their money, voluntarily, not as a requirement. Ananias and Sapphira wanted to keep back some of the money from the sale for themselves, but still wanted everyone to think they'd given the whole amount. What follows may seem quite shocking. The two of them are struck dead by God!

Ananias and Sapphira had been tempted into a mess of corruption. Their love of money had made them keep back some which they should have given to the Church. Their obsession with reputation had driven them to hide that, so that everyone would be impressed by their generosity. And it all led to a huge deceit, which meant they were lying not just to the other believers, but also to God Himself.

CHALLENGE

Is your love of money or reputation leading you into trouble? Do you find yourself lying to cover up your actions? Confess to God now and resolve to put things right with His help.

READ:
1 CHRONICLES 21:1–17

KEY VERSE
v1

'Satan rose up against Israel and caused David to take a census of the people of Israel.'

WHEN I WAS at primary school, we had an older girl assigned to our class on work experience. We loved it when she came outside to play with us at playtime. One day, however, she decided that she didn't want to go outside. Despite the fact that pupils were not allowed to stay in the classroom at playtime, she told a group of us to hide under the table so that we could stay inside, too. Unfortunately, our teacher discovered us hidden under the table and was furious.

Exactly why the census in today's reading was so sinful is not clear. (Perhaps it was a matter of pride for David – seeing just how many people he was leading.) But, crucially, we are told that Satan was the force driving David to take the census. If he had stopped to ask God what He thought of all this, the result might have been very different.

Rather like our work experience student, David was in a position of responsibility. His actions would have consequences for the people of Israel. Perhaps you have areas of responsibility, be that in your family, at school or at church. Do you take this responsibility as seriously as you should?

PRAY

Father God, help me to take my responsibilities seriously. Help me not to be tempted to abuse my position of power, but to carry out my responsibilities in a godly way. Amen.

READ: LUKE 4:1–13

KEY VERSE
v13

'When the devil had finished tempting Jesus, he left him until the next opportunity came.'

WHEN THINKING ABOUT how best to deal with temptation we should of course look to the one person who managed to withstand that temptation; Jesus. The Bible tells us that Jesus was not just fully God, He was also fully man: 'This High Priest of ours understands our weaknesses, for he faced all of the same testings we do, yet he did not sin' (Heb. 4:15). Jesus experienced temptation in just the same way as we do. The crucial difference, though, is that, despite being tempted, He did not give in to it. He did not let it control His thoughts or His actions.

In today's reading we learn about the most famous period of temptation for Jesus. For forty days He was tempted by the devil in the wilderness. So, how does Jesus respond to the temptation He is faced with? Notice that each time the devil tries to tempt Him, Jesus responds with a Bible verse. He arms Himself with truth by quoting scripture, knowing that the devil will have no answer for it. How often when we are tempted do we quote scripture as a way to resist temptation? I suspect for most of us it is not very often. Yet, if this is the example that Jesus sets, then surely it is a strategy worth following.

CHALLENGE

Arm yourself now with Bible verses which you can quote the next time you feel tempted. Perhaps begin with the verses Jesus used in today's reading.

WED 22 JAN

READ: 1 CORINTHIANS 10:1–13

KEY VERSE v13

'When you are tempted, he will show you a way out so that you can endure.'

I HAVE RECENTLY started taking my little boy along to swimming lessons at our local pool. Despite the fact that I go in with him, that he is wearing armbands, and that there are several lifeguards on the side, he is terrified. I tell him over and over again that I won't let him sink to the bottom, but he still worries.

Today's verse should be a source of strength and encouragement to us. Not only does God know and understand the temptations that we face, but He also has the power to ensure that we are not tempted beyond what we can bear.

When we are being tempted, the temptation is often so strong that we fail to stop and think about what other options are open to us. Today's reading tells us that God always gives us a way out. If we stop and listen to what He is telling us when we are being tempted, then He will show us an alternative way.

PRAY

Thank You, Father, that You do not abandon me when I am being tempted. Thank You that you understand what I am going through and that You give me examples of how to cope. Help me to find the way out and avoid giving in to temptation. Amen.

READ:
ROMANS 3:21–26

KEY VERSE
v22

'We are made right with God by placing our faith in Jesus Christ. And this is true for everyone who believes ...'

HAVE YOU EVER had a feeling of guilt hanging over you like a cloud? Last week I told you about the time I broke my camera by opening up the back of it midway through a film. I was so ashamed of what I had done and was too scared to tell anybody. Although it sounds trivial and silly, this guilt really haunted me. It wasn't until several years later, when I confessed what I had done, that I could start to escape from this guilty feeling. Now I still know that I did the wrong thing, but this does not have the same powerful grip on me as it did when it was a secret.

Perhaps there are things that you feel guilty about and struggle to shake from your mind. Today's reading should be a comfort for you. You are not the only one who has sinned. In fact, everybody has done wrong things. But, because of what Jesus did on the cross, we have been set free.

Although we know that God gives us the strength to withstand temptation, we will all, at times, slip up. When this happens, we can go to God, ask for His forgiveness and be confident that He will forgive us.

CHALLENGE

Honesty time. Have you given in to temptation recently? Are you carrying around a load of guilt because of that? Make a decision to turn back to God, admit what you've done, ask His forgiveness and let Him renew your heart and mind.

FRI 24 JAN

READ:
PSALM 73:1–28

KEY VERSE
v13
'Did I keep my heart pure for nothing? Did I keep myself innocent for no reason?'

WHEN HE WAS little, my brother was not a good sleeper. He would get up at night and, when my parents got cross with him, would turn on the charm and say things like, 'I only came to tell Mummy I love her!' In the end, my parents set up a reward chart for him. A week of staying in bed was rewarded with chocolate. I was outraged – I always stayed in bed sensibly and I never got any chocolate!

We often hear about people who do wrong and get away with it. Perhaps they die before anybody finds out. Perhaps they flee the country and are able to live elsewhere. In life, people do get away with things that we feel they should be punished for. Perhaps those who do wrong get rich and live long, happy lives, whilst those who always try and do the right thing struggle with very little to live on.

The psalmist shares our frustration about this: '... I tried to understand why the wicked prosper. But what a difficult task it is!' (v16). We might then ask, what is the point in resisting temptation? But God sees how these people behave and He does not turn a blind eye to it. When we resist temptation, God notices it and He will reward it.

THINK

Do you ever feel resentful about doing the right thing and not being rewarded? Talk to God about that and choose to trust Him to treat you fairly.

READ:
ACTS 26:1–18

KEY VERSE
V1

'Then Agrippa said to Paul, "You may speak in your defense."'

PT1 APOLOGETICS

WE FIND PAUL as a prisoner, on trial for the third time and in danger of being sentenced to death because of his beliefs. In this highly-charged atmosphere, Paul is given the chance to speak in his own defence. He speaks calmly, rationally, drawing on his experiences and setting out reasons for his faith in God.

The word 'Apologetics' might suggest saying sorry for something. Actually, that's the last thing it means! Apologetics means speaking in your defence, as Paul does, giving clear and rational reasons for what you

CONTINUED»

CONTINUED

believe. Or perhaps apologetics just doesn't inspire you. Maybe it seems like a dry, academic exercise, which only causes arguments. Well, you'd be right to point out that intellectual discussions on their own won't convince someone to become a Christian. That will only happen if the Holy Spirit is working in their heart at the same time. But we're living in a world in which atheists and people of other faiths are very clear indeed on what they believe and why they believe it. If we can't explain what we believe and why, we're likely to look very foolish. Apologetics is really important. It isn't about starting an argument. It's about being ready to explain our beliefs when someone asks.

In this series of readings, we'll cover reasons for believing in God, evidence for the life, death and resurrection of Jesus, why the Bible is reliable and some answers for the common questions atheists ask. That's a lot of ground to cover, so we'll take the next two editions of *Mettle* to do it!

THINK

What do you think of apologetics? Whatever your views are, keep an open mind and let God speak to you, challenge you and guide your thinking.

READ: JOHN 1:1–18

KEY VERSE v1

'In the beginning the Word already existed. The Word was with God, and the Word was God.'

MON 27 JAN

I'LL LET YOU into a little secret. Although I'm well into my 30s, I still own a teddy bear. When I've had a tough day, it makes me feel a little better to hide in bed and cuddle something warm and fuzzy. (Promise you won't tell anyone?) I realise it's silly, obviously. I know that, sooner or later, I need to leave the bear, get out of bed and start facing my problems.

Believing in Jesus isn't just a nice idea to make you feel warm and fuzzy. It makes sense. John describes Jesus as the 'Word'. In the original Greek, the word is *Logos*. It conveys logic and rational thought. God isn't an impersonal force, and He doesn't just give us a warm, fuzzy feeling. He thinks things through. The world has order and pattern because of God's rational intelligence.

If God embodies this kind of intelligence, we should show it, too. In a society full of different belief systems, it isn't enough for us to treat our faith like a teddy bear, hide under the duvet and enjoy feeling warm and fuzzy. Our faith must have a solid, rational basis, too, and we must be ready to have some calm, rational discussions with people who disagree with us.

CHALLENGE

How willing are you to let your faith be challenged by differing views? Don't be afraid of this. Your faith won't collapse just because someone disagrees with you. Following Jesus makes sense!

TUES 28 JAN

READ:

2 TIMOTHY 4:1–5

KEY VERSE

v2

'Preach the word of God. Be prepared, whether the time is favorable or not.'

I WAS IN the pub, waiting to be served. While I was waiting, a friend arrived and stood at the bar next to me. We exchanged the usual pleasantries and then there was a lull in the conversation. After a pause, my friend was the next to speak.

'Why are we here?' he asked. I wasn't expecting this, but it was an opportunity to share my faith. So I mentally said a lightning-fast prayer, opened my mouth and went for it.

We can never anticipate when we will get opportunities like this. Our friends won't just want to talk about God at times when we feel ready. The conversation could come any time, whether you're prepared or not. I think this is why Paul urges us to be ready to share what we believe, 'whether the time is favorable or not'. An important step in this is to know what you believe and why. (We've mentioned that already.) On top of that, we need a little courage to open our mouths and say what we really think. And while we're at it, we must remember to be patient and respectful in how we do that (v2). The person asking the question might be aggressive, but God wants us to respect them and their views, even if they don't seem to respect us.

PRAY

Ask God for three things: opportunities to share your faith, the courage to take those opportunities and the patience to be gentle and respectful to whoever's asking the question.

READ: ROMANS 12:1–8

KEY VERSE v2

'Do not conform to the pattern of this world, but be transformed by the renewing of your mind.' (NIV)

APOLOGETICS ISN'T JUST for people with big mouths and degrees in Theology. Not all of us are built that way. God can speak His truth through each of us, however outgoing or clever we think we are. 'The renewing of your mind' means developing more godly attitudes towards yourself, other people and life as a whole. But it also means growing in godly wisdom. Some of us might be stronger than others in gathering intellectual knowledge, but godly wisdom is available to us all. As we commit ourselves to God and get closer to Him, He gives us more and more of His wisdom.

Because of this, we can all give reasons for what we believe. God can still speak through us and give us the ability to explain ourselves. He won't make all of us intellectually brilliant, but He will give all of us insights into who He is and what it means to follow Him. We can also contribute to this process by being careful about what we let into our minds. Steering clear of films, magazines and websites that are likely to influence us badly is a good start. Then, making a conscious effort to read and listen to stuff that will make us wiser and more godly is helpful, too.

CHALLENGE

Don't try to use your personality or your level of education as an excuse for keeping quiet. If someone asks you what you believe, speak up!

THURS 30 JAN

READ:
PSALM 19:1–6

KEY VERSE
v1

'The heavens proclaim the glory of God. The skies display his craftsmanship.'

A COMMON QUESTION we'll encounter is: how do we know that God exists? This Psalm gives us one reason for believing in Him. The whole of creation has God's fingerprints on it. If we look at the world around us, we can see how amazingly detailed and beautiful and vibrant it is. A flea can jump 150 times its own length and pull 160,000 times its own weight. 5 trillion hydrogen atoms can fit onto a pinhead. The human eye can see up to 10 million different colours. It's absolutely mind-boggling. It just doesn't make sense to believe that a world like this simply 'happened'. The world is such an amazing place because our Creator God is behind it all, creating and sustaining it.

Atheist thinkers have challenged this idea. As Douglas Adams once asked, 'Isn't it enough to see that a garden is beautiful without having to believe that there are fairies at the bottom of it too?' But God is no mere fairy. He's the gardener. If the garden is beautiful, it's because God nurtures it.

Atheists may also challenge us for believing in something that we cannot physically see. But just as we cannot see the wind but we can see its effects; we can see the wonders of creation as living evidence of God's great and wonderful power.

THINK
When you look at the world around you, what do you see which makes you believe God created it?

READ: ISAIAH 6:1-8

KEY VERSE v1

'... I saw the Lord. He was sitting on a lofty throne, and the train of his robe filled the Temple.'

SOMEONE ONCE SAID that, rather like chocolate, God is better experienced than explained. A very compelling reason for believing in God is experiencing His presence in a powerful way, which is exactly what happens to Isaiah here. This kind of encounter with God can transform the way we think, speak and act. But of course, for an atheist to have an encounter with God, they would have to at least be open to the possibility of that happening! However, if you have a friend who is an atheist, do not lose hope for them and do not stop praying. After all, our all-powerful God can soften the hardest hearts and open the eyes of the blind.

We can't rely totally on subjective evidence like this to justify our belief in God, though. People also claim to have had 'encounters' with ghosts and aliens and are utterly convinced that these things are real. Unfortunately, there is no way we can conclusively 'prove' that God exists. That would only be possible if God revealed Himself to the entire world, which would leave us no choice but to believe in Him. God loves us too much to force us to follow Him. He conceals Himself and leaves us with a choice: will we choose to have faith and love Him?

PRAY

Lord God, thank You for letting me choose whether to follow You. Please strengthen my faith and help me to love You. Amen.

WEEKEND

1/2 FEB

READ:

DEUTERONOMY 6:1–9

KEY VERSE

v5

'... you must love the LORD your God with all your heart, all your soul, and all your strength.'

IMAGINE TELLING ANOTHER person, 'You must love me'. You'd come across as more than a little bit strange; insecure, controlling, desperate even. I wouldn't recommend trying it as a chat-up line. So how can God say that to us? How can He insist that we love Him? Is God just insecure? And surely, if you command someone to love you, they won't truly love you as a result of this. Love that's forced isn't love at all.

Perhaps it would help to put this chapter from Deuteronomy in context. God is speaking to His people; a people who He created, chose, rescued from slavery and loves deeply. God's commands in this chapter are reinforcing a relationship that already exists between Him and His people. The insistence that they should love Him is a preface to a long and extremely detailed list of laws and commands which God wants His people to keep. The point of the command to love God is that the people's obedience to these laws should spring from a loving relationship with Him, not just from a sense of duty. The people's love for God is not forced, but a response to what God has already done for them. Because He has created, chosen and saved them, they should respond with gratitude, love and total devotion to Him.

Those of us who call ourselves Christians are God's people too, and the same truth applies to us. God has created, chosen and saved us, and He created us for a loving relationship with Him. He urges us to love and worship Him, not because He's insecure or controlling, but because He wants us to follow Him out of love, not just out of duty.

PRAY

Lord, help me to love You with everything I've got. Help me to love You as You love me, and let that motivate my words and actions. Amen.

MON 3 FEB

READ:
EXODUS 20:1–6

KEY VERSE
v5

'... I, the LORD your God, am a jealous God who will not tolerate your affection for any other gods.'

NOBODY LIKES BEING called 'jealous' these days. If you said your boyfriend or girlfriend was jealous, everyone would think they were suspicious, controlling, insecure and unstable. So when we read this key verse, that's probably the impression most of us get of God.

In fact, 'jealous' is probably a bad translation of the original Hebrew text. 'Jealous' implies something extremely negative. 'Zealous' or even 'passionate' might be a better translation. What God wants His people to understand is that He is deeply, passionately committed to them. He wants to emphasise the strength of His love for them and the profound, exclusive relationship He has with them. He insists that Israel should worship no other gods, because He expects Israel to be as committed to this relationship as He is.

Again, this is a truth which applies to us today. God is not 'jealous' in the sense of being controlling, suspicious or vindictive. He loves us passionately, He is totally committed to us and He wants us to love Him with the same devotion and exclusivity He shows us.

THINK
Reflect on the truth that God is deeply, passionately committed to you. How can you show God the same kind of devotion He shows you?

READ: GENESIS 6:5-8

KEY VERSE v7

'And the LORD said, "I will wipe this human race I have created from the face of the earth. Yes, and I will destroy every living thing ..."'

AS WE READ the story of Noah, it's easy to skim over the verses at the start. If we take time over reading these verses, they make highly uncomfortable reading. The prospect of God wiping out the entire human race seems monstrous. Bible passages like these lead some people to the conclusion that God is a tyrant. For example, Richard Dawkins presents a particularly harsh portrait of God:

'The God of the Old Testament is ... a petty, unjust, unforgiving control-freak; a vindictive, bloodthirsty ethnic cleanser; a misogynistic, homophobic, racist, infanticidal, genocidal, filicidal, pestilential, megalomaniacal, sadomasochistic, capriciously malevolent bully.'[1]

This is an extremely strident claim. But quite apart from the theological problem of judging God based on human moral standards, this claim doesn't take into account the context in which this chapter from Genesis was written. It helps to bear in mind just how corrupt the world had become. Humanity was by now 'consistently and totally evil' (v5). Our perfect God was unable to bear this kind of evil, so had little option but to wipe it out, even though it 'broke his heart' (v6) to do that. Our God is not a tyrant, but a righteous judge.

PRAY

Ask God to help you grasp how He can be totally loving and totally holy at the same time.

1. Richard Dawkins, *The God Delusion* (London: Black Swan, 2006) p51.

READ:
DEUTERONOMY 7:1–6

KEY VERSE
v2

'When the LORD your God hands these nations over to you and you conquer them, you must completely destroy them.'

ON 16TH MARCH 1190, a wave of violence against Jews culminated in approximately 150 Jewish men, women and children taking refuge in York castle. Crowds of townspeople surrounded the building, making it impossible for those inside to leave. The castle was set on fire and in the aftermath, all but a few of the Jews were dead. Most unsettling of all, the townspeople seem to have been motivated in their violence by the desire to force the Jews to convert to Christianity.

There are a number of shameful incidents like this in our history. Critics of Christianity or of religion in general would claim that organised religion inevitably leads to violence and persecution. They might even claim that God endorses this behaviour, pointing to passages like Deuteronomy 7 as evidence. But once again, the context of this chapter is crucial. We must bear in mind that some of the nations God was giving to His people were utterly depraved. Worship of pagan gods in this period even included child sacrifice (see Leviticus 20)! God urges His people to end this kind of evil.

Whatever the failings of His people, God is not bloodthirsty. He is an overwhelming force for good against the powers of evil and He brings order, peace and security.

THINK
How would you explain violence which is motivated by religion? Does God endorse this? If not, why does it go on?

READ: JEREMIAH 4:1–8

KEY VERSE v8

'So put on clothes of mourning and weep with broken hearts, for the fierce anger of the LORD is still upon us.'

UNFORTUNATELY THERE'S NO getting away from the fact that there are things which make God angry. In these verses, we see a very powerful – almost shocking – description of God's anger. But once again, it would be a gross distortion of God's character to call Him sadistic or vindictive. God has good reason to be angry in this situation. The people of Israel and Judah know very well how God has provided for them and protected them in the past, but they have chosen to ignore Him and worship other gods instead.

The people go through the motions of worshipping God, but their hearts aren't in it. They're not interested in what God really wants from them and can't be bothered to obey His commands. They worship God in the Temple but forget about Him as soon as they walk out the door. And, as we read on in Jeremiah, we find that God's people are cheating one another and exploiting the poor, while making themselves richer. God is angry, not out of spite at being ignored, but because in turning their backs on Him, His people are harming both themselves and other people. It is God's deep concern for the wellbeing of His people and justice for the vulnerable which rouses His anger.

CHALLENGE

In what situations do you see people harming themselves and others? What could you do about one of these situations? Ask for God's help with this.

FRI 7 FEB

READ:
AMOS 5:18–27

KEY VERSE
v21

'I hate all your show and pretense – the hypocrisy of your religious festivals and solemn assemblies.'

I ONCE HAD a conversation with a friend who had once been a Christian but had recently turned away from the faith. I don't know what his real reasons were for that, but the reason he gave me was quite simple: 'God hates it when we worship Him. So why should I bother?!'

It was this verse from Amos which my friend used to back up his argument. At first glance, this does seem a strange thing for God to say. It's even more shocking in the NIV translation, which puts it: 'I hate, I despise your religious festivals; your assemblies are a stench to me'. If this really was a direct message from God to us today, there probably wouldn't be any point in worshipping Him!

My friend was missing the point. Again, this is all about the context this chapter was written in. Amos was writing to a nation who worshipped God with their words but ignored Him with their hearts and their lifestyle. God doesn't hate our worship in itself. But He does hate it when we just go through the motions of worshipping Him. In John 4:23 it says that God is 'looking' for those who are 'true worshipers', who 'worship the Father in spirit and in truth'.

CHALLENGE

Do you worship God with your words, your heart and your lifestyle? Is there anything you regularly say or do which you know doesn't fit with a worshipping lifestyle?

READ:
PSALM 146:1–10

KEY VERSE
V5

'... joyful are those who have the God of Israel as their helper, whose hope is in the LORD their God.'

HOPE PT1

IT'S INCREDIBLE HOW often we use the word 'hope' in our everyday conversations. As I write we're surrounded by snow and without fail every person who has come into the office today has made an expression of hope that the snow would be gone soon because they need to get to some place or other. We talk about our hopes for all kinds of things - for our holidays, for the future, for exam results, or even our hopes about what might be for tea tonight. What

CONTINUED»

CONTINUED

marks this kind of hope out is that it is mostly dealing with uncertainty and in fact a lot of it can be summed up as wishful thinking!

Christian hope is a different thing altogether. Christian hope, according to the Bible, is not just about wishing that something would happen but having the absolute confidence that it will happen. It's also more about who we have our hope *in* rather than what we're hoping *for*. Through this series of readings we'll be looking at the nature of Christian hope – what it is, how we get it and how we can share it.

In today's reading, the writer of this psalm is reminding himself that while it's very tempting to put his hope in other people, it's foolish to do so as they are no more able to make things happen than he is – after all they are human, too. He tells himself again the story of who God is, the things that God has done in the past, the things that He is currently doing, and the things that He will go on to do. The psalmist knows that God is the only one who we can put our absolute confidence in, and his song of praise encourages us to remember this truth.

THINK

What does having hope in God mean to you? If you were to remind yourself of the things that God has done, what would you include?

READ: ROMANS 8:18–25

KEY VERSE v24

'We were given this hope when we were saved. (If we already have something, we don't need to hope for it.)'

I HAVE A friend who is training to run a marathon. She goes out three or four times a week, running distances that I would need to get a bus for. When I ask her if she thinks she will be able to complete the 26 miles, she responds, 'I have to hope and believe that I can'. She doesn't yet know if it will be possible as runners are encouraged not to run the full distance before the race, but she's hoping, and feeling fairly confident, that on the day she will make the distance.

Marathon runners need to have confidence and expectation or else it makes running the race pointless. This is very much like Christian hope. In this passage Paul tells us that we are living out our life on earth in the hope that one day we will live forever with God in heaven. He says that what we know and experience of God now is just a tiny glimpse of what it will be like when we are face to face with Him, but we can live with absolute confidence and expectation that that day will come. We can have that confidence because, unlike the marathon runner, it's not about us hoping that we can do our best – we can be confident in our hope because of what Jesus has already done.

PRAY

Thank You Lord that we can live with absolute confidence and expectation that You will do what You have said You will do. Amen.

TUES 11 FEB

READ:
ISAIAH 9:1–7

KEY VERSE
v2

'The people who walk in darkness will see a great light. For those who live in a land of deep darkness, a light will shine.'

A FEW YEARS ago I went to Sudan to run some training for people working in displacement camps. Amongst others, one of the sessions that I was asked to deliver was 'Counselling children through war'. I had to get back to the organisers to say that I really couldn't talk about this subject as I had no experience of it. Sudan is a country that for years has known unrest and war. Most of the people I met there had lost family members. They were living in a place where death had cast its shadow.

The situation was very similar for the people that Isaiah was speaking to in today's passage. The people of Judah thought God had forgotten them because of the traumatic situation they were in. Isaiah's word spoke certain hope to them that God had not forgotten them, and that what He had planned was way beyond what they could imagine. They could have confident hope that their despair would not go on forever.

While war continues today, we know that Jesus has come as light into a dark place, and we have confident hope that one day He will come again and end all darkness completely.

PRAY

Jesus, thank You that You have come to bring light into the darkness. I pray today for people who are caught up in war. Please would You give them hope that Your light will come. Amen.

READ:
ROMANS 5:1–8

KEY VERSE
v5

'And this hope will not lead to disappointment. For we know how dearly God loves us, because he has given us the Holy Spirit ...'

WED 12 FEB

WHEN WE HAVE been let down by people in the past, we can begin to believe that all hope leads to disappointment. But hope in God is very different. Hoping for something usually means something that will happen in the future, but Christian hope actually started in the past – with the death and resurrection of Jesus. When the Bible talks about hope, it's talking about us knowing that we are right with God. So, if someone says that they have 'put their hope in God', it's really another way of saying 'I am a Christian'.

One day I will stand before God and give an account for my life. If I have put my hope in God, I can have hope that when I stand before Him it will all be OK because Jesus, who died on the cross for me, will be there with me. It's not about wishing that He will save us - Paul wants us to know in this passage that Jesus definitely has saved us! I don't have to fear – my hope won't be disappointed because it's an absolute certainty. And I can know this for sure because God has given me the Holy Spirit so that I would truly know His love and peace.

CHALLENGE

Take some time to think about verse 8, 'But God showed his great love for us by sending Christ to die for us while we were still sinners'. Do disappointments in other people keep you from trusting God? Do you know God's love as a reality?

THURS 13 FEB

READ: ROMANS 8:31–39

KEY VERSE v38

'And I am convinced that nothing can ever separate us from God's love ... not even the powers of hell can separate us from God's love.'

FRIENDSHIPS CAN BE very fragile at times. They can be going along really well and then all of a sudden something happens that changes everything and the friendship is broken. Very few people manage to make it through life with all their friendships intact. Friends come and friends go, whether that's because of a difficult situation or argument, or simply because they move away. We hope that those people who are our friends today will be our friends tomorrow – but there is no guarantee.

Over the years I've met a number of people who feel that their relationship with God is similar. They feel that while things are going well, the relationship is good. But they live in fear that if they do something wrong God will abandon them and not come back. Paul wants us to be absolutely clear that this is not how it is with God. The hope we can have in Him is constant and certain. There is nothing we can do that will make God leave, and there is nothing that can happen that will make Him stop loving us. Christians are not created to live in fear of their relationship with God ending, but in certain hope of God's constant love.

THINK

Who do you know who may be struggling to believe that God loves them? How can you communicate and demonstrate God's love to them?

READ: PHILIPPIANS 3:7–11

KEY VERSE v8

'Yes, everything else is worthless when compared with the infinite value of knowing Christ Jesus my Lord.'

THIS WEEK WE'VE been looking at the nature of Christian hope – we've seen that those who love God and follow Him are able to have confidence in their relationship with God today, and know for certain that they have a future in heaven with Him. Because Jesus died and rose again, our sin no longer separates us from God. We have the certain hope of having been made right with Him.

This knowledge should encourage us in our daily lives. In his letter to the church in Philippi, Paul says that this knowledge has altered the course of his life. All of the things that he used to think were important – his background, his job, how he was thought of – all those things that once gave him confidence and hope, he now thinks of as complete rubbish. Paul has come to know that it's only hope in Jesus that actually matters. A few years later, when he knows his life is coming to an end, he writes to his friend Timothy to let him know that his hope is about to be fulfilled (2 Tim. 4:6–8). Paul knows that he is about to go and be with Christ, and the life that he lived for God had all been worth it.

CHALLENGE

Could you say that, 'everything else is worthless compared with knowing Christ'? Do you ever treat anything else as more important than that?

WEEKEND

15/16 FEB

READ:

PSALM 25:1–22

KEY VERSE

v5

'Lead me by your truth and teach me, for you are the God who saves me. All day long I put my hope in you.'

WHEN I WAS a teenager I used to go to a monthly youth gathering that always ended in exactly the same way, no matter what the theme had been. Whoever was leading the event would conclude by leaning forward over the pulpit, looking us all in the eye, and asking us the heart-searching question, 'If you get hit by a bus on the way home this evening, do you know that you'll be going to heaven?' Now, this question always used to puzzle me because our church was in a little village that wasn't on a bus route, but I'm guessing that wasn't really the point!

Our hope as Christians is about our eternal future – knowing for certain that when we die we will be able to spend eternity with God. However, there is so much more to it than that. The hope that God gives is not just for some future date, it's for now too – it's a hope for the everyday things of our lives. We can talk to God about all the details of our lives and ask Him to show us the way forward, to help us when we don't know what to do, or don't understand what's happening. God wants us to know that He is deeply interested and involved in our lives today and that there is nothing that is beyond His hope.

The Psalms are records of people's prayers about the daily things of their lives as well as about their hope for their future with God. Some are prayers of distress or prayers for help, while others are songs of praise for the things God has done. This psalm asks particularly for guidance and protection. We too can call on God every day, and like the psalmist, we can put our hope in Him all day long.

THINK

As you go through this coming week, think about the things that you are doing, the people you are meeting, and the questions that you are facing and ask God to help you in all those things.

MON 17 FEB

READ:
RUTH 1:1–22

KEY VERSE
v16

'Wherever you go, I will go; wherever you live, I will live. Your people will be my people, and your God will be my God.'

THE STORY OF Ruth is one of the most profound stories of hope that the Bible records for us. In many ways the story should have ended at verse 5 with the death of Naomi's husband and sons. In their culture men were the key players and without them, women had nothing. They had no right to their land and therefore no hope of a future. However, Ruth and Naomi's story continued.

By the end of chapter 1 we find Ruth and Naomi in a hopeless situation. The future looks bleak, yet what unfolds is the most incredible story of God's provision for them. Ruth is from Moab so would have worshipped other gods, but in making her commitment to Naomi she chooses to worship and trust the God of Israel and He doesn't let her down. It's amazing how often the phrase, 'it just so happened' occurs in the story. This is deliberate on the part of the writer – he wants the readers to know that it didn't 'just so happen'. God was at work. He was bringing these women out of such a hopeless situation. And so the story that begins with hopelessness and despair ends with hope and purpose, and these women who had lost everything, become part of the family line of Jesus.

PRAY
Is there a situation that you are feeling hopeless about? Ask God to give you hope in that situation, and to help you see where He is at work.

READ:
1 PETER 1:3–12

KEY VERSE
v3

'It is by his great mercy that we have been born again, because God raised Jesus Christ from the dead. Now we live with great expectation ...'

I HAVE ALWAYS been hugely challenged by stories of Christians who live in parts of the world where it's very difficult to follow Jesus. Even today, people are risking their lives because of their faith and face imprisonment or worse on a regular basis. Yet they are people of incredible hope. This is because they understand something of what Peter is writing about in this letter.

The Christian life is a life that is full of hope, but that doesn't mean it's without its trials and difficult times. The people to whom Peter was writing were experiencing persecution for their faith but Peter wanted them to know that they could still hold onto hope, that in fact they could know real joy in that situation because of the hope they have. We may not be facing such severe persecution but we will still face difficult times and Peter's message is the same for us. Even in the midst of difficulties we can have hope and experience joy, and even find that our faith is strengthened through these times. However bleak life looks at the moment, we can live with expectation, knowing that God is with us and that our destiny is to be with Him for eternity.

CHALLENGE

What do you know about Christians who are being persecuted in different parts of the world? Try to find out about a particular situation and write a letter to encourage believers there.

READ:
LUKE 24:13–34

KEY VERSE
v32

'... "Didn't our hearts burn within us as he talked with us on the road and explained the Scriptures to us?"'

IF EVER THERE was a picture of hopelessness, it's the picture of these two people making their way to Emmaus following the death of Jesus. We can't imagine what they must have been feeling – their whole world had just been turned upside down, captured in the words of verse 21, 'We had hoped he was the Messiah who had come to rescue Israel'. They had followed Jesus, seen Him do incredible things, listened to His life-changing teaching and put all their hope in Him, believing that He was the one the prophets had written of long ago. But now that had all changed. They'd seen Jesus arrested, beaten and nailed to a cross, and as the stone sealed the tomb where He lay dead, so their hopes had died, too.

It was in the midst of their sadness and despair that Jesus came and met with them. Interestingly, they didn't recognise Him at first. Yet as Jesus talked with them, 'their eyes were opened' (v31) and hope was rekindled. Jesus was alive, and that changed everything! Re-vitalised with hope, they ran the distance back to Jerusalem to share the news with the others. Jesus is still alive today in us and through us He can open the eyes of those who have yet to find Him.

CHALLENGE

Are you in a situation that makes you feel doubtful or hopeless? Read this passage again and ask God to remind you of the hope that He has given you.

READ: PSALM 31:9–24

KEY VERSE v24

'So be strong and courageous, all you who put your hope in the LORD!'

BEN HAD HIS heart set on going on a gap year mission trip. It was something he'd dreamt about for years and it finally felt like it was going to happen. He had passed his interview, his funding had been raised and all that was left was for a church leader to give him a reference. Sadly this is where it all fell apart. The main church leader who knew Ben well was away when the request came in, so another leader wrote it and told the organisation that Ben wasn't very well known at the church, and so they couldn't endorse his involvement. Ben was gutted. In one moment it all came to an end and he felt utterly shattered.

Over the coming months, Ben spent a lot of time praying about what had happened and really felt that God knew his disappointment and how his hopes had been brought crashing down. Instead of allowing the situation to make him bitter, he committed himself to serving more at church, and the following year he was able to join the gap year team.

Sometimes things don't go the way we'd hoped. What we do in these moments is extremely important. The psalmist and Ben show us that we can go to God with our disappointment, and ask Him to help us and to give us strength to continue.

THINK

How do you respond when you face disappointment, particularly when it's because of something that someone else has or hasn't done?

FRI 21 FEB

READ:
PSALM 42:1–11

KEY VERSES
vv5–6

'Why am I discouraged? Why is my heart so sad? I will put my hope in God! I will praise him again – my Savior and my God!'

YESTERDAY WE SAW that sometimes disappointments come from things or people outside of our control. Sometimes, however, we just find ourselves feeling a bit down and short of hope. The writer of today's psalm is certainly experiencing that. He's remembering how things used to feel when his relationship with God felt full of life, but now those feelings seem to have gone.

A while ago my five-year-old goddaughter was having a tantrum because things weren't going her way. Just as she was getting really wound up, she stopped and looked at me and said, 'I think I need to go and have a word with myself'. I was amazed at her ability to recognise this and very impressed as she took herself off to sort herself out! It appears to me that this is what the psalmist is doing – he recognises that he's feeling down, but rather than getting deeper into hopelessness, he tells God very clearly how he's feeling and talks to himself, to his heart and reminds himself to keep putting his hope back in God. And then he does the best thing we can do when feeling discouraged – he praises God, choosing to remember who God is and to worship Him for it.

PRAY

Is there something that you are feeling down about? Tell God how you feel, and remind yourself about how good God is.

WEEKEND 22/23 FEB

READ: REVELATION 2:7

KEY VERSE V7

'Anyone with ears to hear must listen to the Spirit and understand what he is saying to the churches.'

THE CHURCH PT2

OVER THE NEXT fortnight we'll be looking at the book of Revelation and what it has to say about the Church. The book was written to seven churches in Asia, partly to instruct them in the ways they should behave. Each of the seven churches is mentioned specifically at the start of the book with constructive comments and instructions about how they can change for the better.

The book of Revelation is full of symbols and pictures

CONTINUED

CONTINUED

to describe things and therefore is not the easiest part of the Bible to understand. The number seven is used a lot throughout the whole of the Bible and is meant to symbolise completeness and wholeness. It was seen as the perfect number. Therefore, although the book is addressed to seven specific churches, it can be read as a message to the Church as a whole as well. There is much that we can take from the book to show us how the Church and the people within it should act.

The verse we have read today reflects how John, the writer, finishes off each section to one of the churches. John is saying that they need to look to the Holy Spirit to receive guidance on how they should live and act.

God's Spirit is with us to guide us in the right ways. We need to set aside time to listen to Him and find out what He is saying to us. He may tell us that we are doing well or He may convict us that the things we are doing are not right and we need to change. Also, He may tell us to do new things. Most importantly we should be willing to listen and hear what the Spirit is saying – and then act on what He says to us.

PRAY

Spend some time now listening to God's Spirit. It may be hard to start with but ask God to speak and then be patient and sit and listen to what He has to say.

READ: REVELATION 2:1–7

KEY VERSE
v4

'But I have this complaint against you. You don't love me or each other as you did at first!'

THE CHURCH IN Ephesus was a hardworking and enduring church. The believers didn't tolerate sin or listen to false teaching. But John says that the Spirit has something to say to them – they need to avoid becoming complacent and used to their ways.

It would seem that they had lost some of the spark they first had when they became Christians and started to work together. It's an easy thing to do. When you are used to living as a Christian and being in a certain situation within a church, it can just become routine rather than something you do out of love for God. I am sure you can think of times in your life when you've lost your passion or enthusiasm for something. For example, it might be your love of playing in a sports team, or a relationship with a boyfriend or girlfriend which started off really well but then lost its spark and just became dull and ordinary.

Our relationship with God can be exactly the same. It is great to spend time every so often reminding yourself that He loves you and that He died and rose again for you – this is what your relationship is built upon. What we do doesn't affect how much God loves us.

PRAY

Spend time over the coming days thinking about this and praying that God will restore in you the passion you first had for Him.

TUES 25 FEB

READ:
REVELATION 2:8–11

KEY VERSE
v10

'But if you remain faithful even when facing death, I will give you the crown of life.'

THE CHURCH IN Smyrna was a spiritually rich place but it was receiving a lot of persecution from Jews, causing it great trouble and financial poverty. The Spirit knew that they were suffering and that even further and worse suffering was to come. It would mean that some of them would be faced with death because of their faith.

In certain parts of the world today, Christians have to daily face persecution or even death because of what they believe in. We can so easily take it for granted that we can worship God and tell people about Him without facing anything that serious. We may get some taunting and have names thrown at us, but we won't have to die for our faith. What would we do if we lived in a culture where we had the choice of our life or our belief in God? I would like to think that I would be strong-willed enough to stick to my beliefs – but would I? Would you?

Is God that important to you that you would remain faithful even when facing death? Would you be able to put up with a life like that?

THINK

Spend some time thinking about this and the importance your beliefs have in your life. Is God so important to you that you would be willing to face persecution and suffering, whatever form that might take in your own situation?

READ:
REVELATION 2:12–17

KEY VERSES
vv15-16

'... you have some Nicolaitans among you who follow the same teaching. Repent of your sin ...'

WED 26 FEB

THE CHURCH IN Pergamum had stayed faithful and loyal even when people had been martyred for their beliefs there. However, they were tolerating people in their church who were following false teaching and committing sins against the church. They were relaxing the ways in which they thought they ought to live. The Spirit was telling them to repent and come back to Him.

Something we need to be aware of is that, even if we sin, God is always there, waiting for us to come back. We just need to make a decision to live differently in the future, tell Him that we are sorry and He will forgive us. In this account, the Spirit offers forgiveness, symbolised here as white stones, to those who repent. At that time, if someone was on trial, they would be given a black stone if they were found guilty and white if they were allowed to go free.

The Spirit is saying that if they repent of the sins they have committed they will be set free. God longs to set us free from the sins we commit. He doesn't want them to have a hold over us in any way. This passage also shows us that we need to be aware of God's judgment if we do not come back to Him.

PRAY

Take some time to thank God for His amazing grace, which is always available to set us free from our sin. Pray that He will help you to not fall into the trap of having a relaxed attitude to sin.

THURS 27 FEB

READ:
REVELATION 2:18–29

KEY VERSES
VV 24–25

'I will ask nothing more of you except that you hold tightly to what you have until I come.'

THE CHURCH IN Thyatira had shown a great love of God through its service and endurance. However, it was struggling because a woman in the church was giving them false teaching and leading them into a lifestyle of sexual sin and idol worship. But there were some in the church who had not given in to this false teaching and the Spirit was urging them to stay strong in their correct beliefs and behaviour.

So often when we are faced with a decision it is easier to follow the crowd and not stick to what we actually believe in. Whether it is lying to your parents about something, giving in to temptations you struggle with – such as smoking or drinking – or going that little bit too far with your boyfriend or girlfriend. You may think that to go along with any of these things just seems normal. Yes, if you're found out, there might be some consequences, but you persuade yourself that none of these things are really that bad. However, if we begin to compromise even in small things, we can find ourselves turning our backs on God.

CHALLENGE

What would happen if you stuck to what was right and true, even if that meant standing out from the crowd? The Holy Spirit asked one thing of the people in Thyatira: to hold tightly to what they knew to be true. How far can you say that you do that?

READ: REVELATION 3:1–6

KEY VERSE v2

'Wake up! Strengthen what little remains, for even what is left is almost dead.'

THE CHURCH IN Sardis had a really good past and a reputation for being strong and alive in its worship of God. However, things had started to go downhill and the people had started to commit sinful acts.

Again, as we have seen with some of the other churches described in Revelation, they were asked to repent and return to God. He asked them to strengthen the good qualities they had, to build themselves up again and to remember what they were like when they first believed.

Something that can be a problem in the Christian life is that people can 'fall asleep'. They can lose sight of God's goals for them as a person and as a church. We can go through all the motions of church and the Christian life but it can end up being half-hearted. As others can't always recognise this in us, just as the church in Sardis had a false 'reputation for being alive', we must remember to question our own hearts.

Jesus asks for our all, not just a small attempt at living for Him. He wants us to live for Him in a fully awake, joyful and wholehearted way.

THINK

How do you live for Christ in each area of your life, now? Can you pinpoint a time when you were perhaps more wholehearted in your attitudes in these areas? Pray that God will help you to restore this wholehearted attitude.

WEEKEND

1/2 MAR

READ:

REVELATION 3:7–13

KEY VERSE

v8

'I know all the things you do ... You have little strength, yet you obeyed my word and did not deny me.'

THE CHURCH IN Philadelphia was small and weak, yet they have come through persecution and trials, remaining faithful to God and their beliefs. They were being asked to remain faithful and to realise that God had noticed everything they had done.

It is an amazing fact that whatever we do – whether in thought, word or action – God knows about it. Anything that may go unnoticed by others, God sees and acknowledges. God was pleased with the church in Philadelphia and what they had done. I wonder what God thinks of me or you and the things we have done? Would He be pleased or would it be one of those times when we are told: 'Could do better'? At school it always feels really good to get an A or B grade, but sometimes when we get lower grades, that's just what our teachers or parents tell us : 'You could do better'. This can make us feel really bad, especially when we've been working really hard, aiming to do our best.

God loves everything we do in His name, however big or small it may be. It can make the world of difference to Him and He can use anything we offer. Yes, at times He may think (and so may we) that we 'could do better' but He will still use what we offer for His glory. But, just like this church, He asks us to persevere in His name and keep going, because He has set us free to know Him and be with Him.

CHALLENGE

Take time this weekend to think and pray about what you offer to God and your church. Over this week we've looked at many areas and issues the Holy Spirit was highlighting to the churches for improvement. What has spoken to you? In which areas of your life can you improve? The book of Revelation is just as relevant now to your situation as it was when it was first written.

MON 3 MAR

READ:
REVELATION 3:14–22

KEY VERSE
v17

'You say, "… I don't need a thing!" … you don't realize that you are wretched and miserable and poor and blind and naked.'

THE CHURCH IN Laodicea was the last of the seven churches addressed. The people of the church were rich and had always had everything they wanted, but now they were getting complacent. They were like 'lukewarm water' – they were on the fence with God, not fully following or relying on Him. While God was knocking at their door, they were too concerned with their wealth to hear. The Holy Spirit tried to point out to them that although they might have thought they had everything they needed, there is more to life than being rich. God could provide a richness that was purer than they could ever have hoped for.

We can easily become blinded to the things we need help with. If we live in a comfortable situation, it's quite hard to accept that we need anything at all. What we need to realise is that God wants to provide us with everything we need. As it says in 2 Corinthians 12:10: 'For when I am weak, then I am strong.' Through our weakness, God can be strong in our lives, and through Him we can be stronger than we could ever be on our own. God wants us to turn away from the blindness of seeing things the way the world does and instead to see things His way.

CHALLENGE
Think about this in relation to yourself and your church. Are you getting complacent? Do you need to accept you are weak in order for God to make you strong?

READ:
REVELATION 12:1–18

KEY VERSE
v1

'I saw a woman clothed with the sun, with the moon beneath her feet, and a crown of twelve stars on her head.'

MOVING AWAY FROM the seven churches, there is more imagery and symbolism in Revelation about the Church. Chapter 12 tells the story of how the devil will persecute the Church.

The woman described, and her children, represent the believers of Jesus – the Church. The 12 stars on her head represent the tribes of Israel from the Old Testament, one of which Jesus was descended from. Her first baby is Jesus, who goes up to heaven to be with God after the dragon (the devil) tries to defeat Him and fails. It is hard to grasp all the symbolism, but the basic idea is that the Church will have to go through hardships and persecution because of the devil trying to defeat it.

In the middle of the story are three verses which cry out Jesus in joy and praise because He has defeated the enemy. What we need to remember when looking at all these complex images is that God has things under control. He knows what is going on and what is still to happen. All we need to know is that the victory has already been won. The devil has been defeated and however hard life and being a Christian may seem to get, God is faithful to us and won't let us go.

PRAY

Praise and thank God for what He has done for His Church by defeating the enemy. Ask Him to help you persevere when times are hard.

WED 5 MAR

READ:
REVELATION 19:1–10

KEY VERSE
v6

'Then I heard again what sounded like the shout of a vast crowd or the roar of mighty ocean waves ... "Praise the Lord!"'

WHAT AN AMAZING day this will be! All believers will be there to praise and worship. The Church together, finally united in the one thing that is common to all its parts – their love of God. Finally we will be able to praise and worship because God is reigning and everything has been brought to perfection. Verse 7 goes on to tell us about the wedding that we will be a part of. This shows us the close relationship between God and His people – that the Church is finally being fully united to Him.

In verse 8 we see that God has given the Bride the gift of His holiness, seen in the form of fine white linen. This is in return for the work the believers have been doing in God's name. They have been preparing themselves for this day by living for Him.

Are you preparing for this day? We know the Bible says it is not by works that we are saved but by God's grace (Eph. 2:8–9), but we need to be prepared and ready for what is coming. Out of our love for God we should want to do what will please Him. Are we living our lives as God wants us to so that we too can receive His gift of holiness?

CHALLENGE

Think about how you are living your life. Is it in a way that shows God you want to be part of this crowd saying 'Hallelujah'? Are you living with a heavenly focus or an earthly focus?

READ:
REVELATION 21:3–4

KEY VERSE
v3

'Look, God's home is now among his people! He will live with them, and they will be his people.'

THURS 6 MAR

THE KEY VERSE today describes the final part of God's union with the Church. The new Jerusalem, the holy city, has come down from heaven from God (v2). God and His people can physically live together! There is no barrier or gap between the two, no sin to get in the way. This is what God has made the Church for: to be able, one day, to have this full union with Him.

Verse 4 goes on to tell us there will be no more sorrow or pain or death. All the evil of the world will be gone. All we will know is what it is like to live in complete harmony with God, and the holiness and beauty this will bring about.

What an amazing promise for us to hold onto. It is easy sometimes to look at the Church and wonder, 'How can anything good come from this? What good is it doing to me?' However, this promise of the new Jerusalem in Revelation shows us that finally all things will be made right and the Church will live with God. He will be among His people. Imagine that amazing new life: there will be none of the pain and sorrow we experience now – God will be living with us and we will see him face to face.

PRAY

Thank and praise God for this promise of the future for you and all His believers. Ask Him to keep reminding you of the promise that, as part of His Body, you will be part of an amazing future.

FRI 7 MAR

READ: REVELATION 22:14–17

KEY VERSE v17

'Let anyone who is thirsty come. Let anyone who desires drink freely from the water of life.'

VERSE 17 TELLS everyone that they can come and receive from God if they want to – His gift is free. Both the Spirit and the Church tell people to come and be believers. Anyone who is thirsty for the life that God gives can come. Are you thirsty for more of God? Are your ears open to hear God's Spirit say, 'Come'?

We can get quite comfortable in our position in life. You may go to church most Sundays, read your Bible and pray to God. On the odd occasion you may even talk to your friends about who God is and what you believe in. Not that any of that is wrong – it is all good and should be part of what you do as a Christian – but there can be so much more than that to knowing God. Just as a groom desires to be with his bride, we should long to be closer to God.

Have you got a real thirst for who God is, for a strong relationship with Him? He longs for us to want more of Him in our lives and to know Him even better than we do now. Do you long for this too? Do you want to be more than a lukewarm Christian, one who wholeheartedly believes in Jesus? Do you want to be a committed part of His Bride, the Church?

PRAY

Ask God to help you to be thirsty for Him and ask for true fellowship with His people, the Church.

READ: JAMES 1:12–18

KEY VERSE V13

'... do not say, "God is tempting me." God is never tempted to do wrong, and he never tempts anyone else.'

TEMPTATION PT2

HOW TO RESIST TEMPTATION

A FEW WEEKS ago we spent some time looking at temptation and focusing on the examples of different people in the Bible who were faced with temptation. Over the next fortnight we return to this issue of temptation but we will be focusing more on some strategies to help us resist temptation.

Spend a few moments thinking about some of your teachers. Some teachers are really supportive, helping you to learn everything that you need to

CONTINUED»

CONTINUED

know and providing valuable guidance in areas that you struggle with. Sometimes, however, we can get teachers who seem to delight in trying to trip us up. Just when we think we've mastered the subject, they spring something else at us, making us feel stupid and inadequate.

In today's reading, James tells us that God is not trying to trick us or trip us up. When we are facing temptation, this is not God trying to catch us out. Temptation comes from our own evil desires, which the devil then takes advantage of. God is certainly not twisted enough to tempt us to do something which He has already forbidden us to do! No. God is not a sadist. He is the source of everything 'good and perfect' (v17).

God is like one of those good teachers who try to help and support us. In fact, He is the greatest Teacher we will ever have! God equips us with tools to help us stand firm when we are tempted, and His reward for our obedience is more than just a shiny sticker – His reward is 'the crown of life' (v12). Over the next fortnight we will look in more depth at the tools we need to help us in our battle against temptation.

PRAY

Thank God for being the source of everything good and perfect and for loving to bless and reward us. Ask for His help and wisdom in resisting temptation.

READ:
LUKE 8:4–15

MON 10 MAR

KEY VERSE
v13

'... But since they don't have deep roots, they believe for a while, then they fall away when they face temptation.'

WHEN I WAS a kid, I sometimes used to grow bulbs in a transparent container. I was fascinated to watch the plant roots growing crazily under the bulb. So often we don't see the roots of a plant, but they play an essential role, helping it to stay firm.

The Parable of the Sower is one of the best known stories from the New Testament. Of course Jesus' real purpose in telling this story is not to give tips to farmers! This parable is all about how deep the roots of our faith are and how these determine our futures.

Jesus tells us that some people do not allow their faith to take deep root. As a consequence, these people are prone to giving way to temptation. In the same way as roots are important in helping a plant to stand firmly in the ground and take up water and nutrients, deep roots are important for growing our faith and preventing us from falling into temptation.

How do we ensure that we develop good roots? Plant roots reach for water and nutrients. We should ensure that we seek to find nourishment for our faith – through meeting with other Christians, praying, and immersing ourselves in God's Word.

THINK

What are your roots like? Will they help to guard you against temptation? How can you strengthen and deepen your roots?

TUES 11 MAR

READ:
PSALM 119:1–16

KEY VERSE
v11

'I have hidden your word in my heart,
that I might not sin against you.'

DO YOU EVER find yourself in situations where you can hear your mum or dad's voice in the back of your head? Perhaps you can imagine them telling you to calm down when you're stressed or to get on with a job when you're being lazy. If we take the messages that they give us to heart, then these may help (or hinder) us, even when they're not with us in person.

When we read about Jesus' temptation in the desert, we saw how He used the words of Scripture to help Him. One of the key things we took away from the story of Jesus' temptation was that He knew Bible verses by heart, and He used these to fight off temptation, even though that temptation might have seemed highly inviting.

A good knowledge of the Bible teaches us to be firmly rooted in what is right and wrong and to understand the way God wants us to live. There's no substitute for a deep understanding of God's Word and His will for our lives. We need to take the time when reading our Bible to not just read it, but take it to heart. As the Bible takes root in our hearts and minds, then we will be armed with power greater than that of temptation.

CHALLENGE

How often do you read the Bible but not really take it in and let it impact the way you think? Spend some time asking God to help you really rejoice in His Word and truly take it to heart.

READ: MATTHEW 26:36–46

WED 12 MAR

KEY VERSE v41

'Keep watch and pray, so that you will not give in to temptation. For the spirit is willing, but the body is weak!'

HAVE YOU EVER fallen asleep without meaning to? My little boy often falls asleep when we're on a long car journey. Sometimes I try and stop him if it's late in the afternoon as I know it will stop him from going to bed later on. I'll tell him to keep his eyes open and try and bribe him to stay awake with the promise of chocolate biscuits. But, no matter how much he wants to stay awake, he usually falls asleep. Just like in today's key verse, 'the spirit is willing, but the body is weak'.

Today's reading contains some of the last words that Jesus would speak to His disciples before His death. Therefore, they are especially significant. He warns them of temptation and provides them with a key strategy to guard them against it, which is to pray.

When we find ourselves in a scary situation, we often say short prayers, asking God to help. We don't always do this when we are tempted, though. Yet as we pray, we are opening ourselves to receive God's strength and putting ourselves in the position where we rely on Him completely. That, of course, is the best place we could possibly be.

PRAY

Father God, please help me in my battle against my wrong desires. Help me to find the strength to resist temptation, to stand firm in my faith, and to do what is right according to Your Word. Amen.

THURS 13 MAR

READ:

NUMBERS 25:1–3

KEY VERSE

v2

'These women invited them to attend sacrifices to their gods, so the Israelites ... worshiped the gods of Moab.'

WE LIVE IN a multi-cultural world, and many of us have friends from different backgrounds and religions. At first glance, today's reading can make it seem as if God is against this. But if we look to the example of Jesus, we see that this is not the case. Jesus spent time with people from all walks of life and, in so doing, showed us that it is good and important to interact with people from different backgrounds.

So, what exactly is the problem in today's reading? It is the fact that the Israelites were being led away from God. They were so enamoured with these women that they started to worship their gods, rather than the one true God.

Peer pressure can have an effect on our relationship with God and the way we live our lives. If we invest all our energy in people who do not know Jesus, then we may find that we are tempted to leave Jesus out of our lives in the same way as these people do. This does not mean that we should not be friends with anyone who isn't a Christian! But it is important to try and foster close friendships with those who share our faith. In doing so, we can help keep each other on the right path.

THINK

Who are the people that you confide in and turn to for advice and guidance? Are they Christians? Do any of your friendships lead to temptation to turn your back on God?

READ:
GALATIANS 6:1–10

KEY VERSE
v1

'... if another believer is overcome by some sin ... gently and humbly help that person back onto the right path ...'

WHEN WE'VE DONE something that we know is wrong, one of the best ways to prevent this from happening again is to confess it to another Christian who cares about you and will ask you in future how you are doing at resisting this temptation. Yes, it can be awkward, but it's a really valuable exercise!

Knowing that we are accountable to someone who wants to help us in our struggles is a great tool for helping us to resist temptation. When we know someone will ask us if we've read the Bible recently, we are more likely to make sure we read it. When we know that someone will ask us if we've looked at dodgy websites recently, we are more likely to be careful about our online behaviour. When we are with those who resist the temptation to gossip, we will be less likely to talk judgingly about someone.

In today's reading, Paul urges us to help and support another with their struggles. But it does highlight a potential problem as well: the danger of falling into the same temptation ourselves. When we try and support another Christian, we must be aware of the devil's attempts to trip us up. We cannot afford to let our guard down.

CHALLENGE

Verse 3 says that we should all be willing to help others in their struggles. Do you think other Christians look up to you as someone they can turn to for help? What sort of example do you set?

WEEKEND

15/16 MAR

READ:

EPHESIANS 6:10–18

KEY VERSE

v11

'Put on all of God's armor so that you will be able to stand firm against all strategies of the devil.'

WE HAVE TALKED a lot about standing firm in the face of temptation. But, of course, this is a lot easier said than done. Imagine you're standing in a field as a hurricane approaches. It would be all very well for me to tell you, 'Stand firm!', but it wouldn't be as easy as I might make it sound! This passage from Ephesians 6 gives us some practical suggestions on how we can equip ourselves so that we are able to stand firm in God.

Take another look at the passage and have a go at putting it into your own words. What is it actually trying to say?

We need to know and be confident in what we believe. God has won the battle against the devil. If we are confident in this, then this will help us stand up to the devil when he tries to lure us into temptation. Reading the Bible regularly and praying are key to developing our relationship with God and understanding and solidifying our faith. As well as this, fellowship with other Christians who can help and support us when we are struggling is vital.

God does not expect us to go out and fight temptation on our own. As we've already learnt, He will not allow us to be tempted beyond what we can bear. If we equip ourselves with the armour He provides, God can work through that to strengthen us as we try to stand firm against temptation. If a soldier goes into battle without any of the equipment provided by his commanding officer, he cannot expect to stay safe from the enemy. Similarly, if we don't use the armour provided by God, we'll have a much harder time resisting temptation.

PRAY

Thank You, Father, that You don't leave us to fend for ourselves but that You provide us with all that we need to stand up to the devil. Help us to remember that You are the ultimate Victor and that we are on the winning side. Amen.

MON 17 MAR

READ:
1 TIMOTHY 6:6–12

KEY VERSE
v9

'But people who long to be rich fall into temptation and are trapped by many foolish and harmful desires ...'

WHAT DO YOU strive for in life? Do you long to be famous? Do you spend hours on end training? Do you obsess over perfecting your hair or make up, trying to be more beautiful? Whatever it is that you hope to be, working towards this ambition can take up a lot of your time and energy.

We can have all sorts of desires and goals and some of these might even be good and noble things. But if we obsess over trying to achieve some worldly goal or ambition – however important it might seem – our focus on God inevitably slips. This then makes us more prone to temptation. As Paul tells Timothy, when we long for money in particular, we can be tempted and 'trapped by many foolish and harmful desires' which can then lead to 'ruin and destruction' (1 Tim. 6:9).

So what should we do? Paul tells Timothy to 'Pursue righteousness and a godly life, along with faith, love, perseverance, and gentleness' (1 Tim. 6:11). Rather than focusing on worldly goals, our ultimate aim should be to live a godly life. We will then be more alert and ready to face temptation. And choosing to be content with what we have is bound to make us happier and more peaceful (v6).

CHALLENGE
Make a list of everything you are thankful for. Thank God for these things. And ask Him to show you if anything is distracting you from Him. Resolve to put Him first.

READ: PHILIPPIANS 4:4–9

KEY VERSE v8

'Fix your thoughts on what is true, and honorable, and right, and pure, and lovely, and admirable.'

HAVE YOU NOTICED that when people hold a certain opinion, the way they see the world serves to confirm their point of view. Someone who believes that young people are all rude and lazy only sees rude and lazy young people – they fail to notice all the lovely young people there are out there!

In today's reading, Paul tells us that we can affect the way our mind works by choosing to focus our thoughts. If you find yourself thinking lustful thoughts, or angry thoughts, or any other sinful thoughts that are a result of temptation, then try redirecting your thoughts. Choose to focus on what is 'true ... honorable and right'.

This comes down to what we choose to let influence us. Avoid films, magazines and websites that you know will feed your temptation. Instead, choose to watch, read and listen to things which will inspire you, fill your head with truth and wisdom, and feed your faith. In this way, God can transform your thinking. You may even find that after a while, some of those old temptations just don't bother you anymore.

THINK

Have you noticed that what you watch, read or listen to affects the way you think, feel or act? What should you stop watching, reading or listening to, because they lead you into temptation? What could you start watching, reading or listening to instead?

WED 19 MAR

READ:
JOHN 10:1–10

KEY VERSE
v10

'The thief's purpose is to steal and kill and destroy.'

I'M NOT A fan of camping. I find it difficult to sleep knowing there is just a bit of canvas between me and the outside world. Every little noise startles me and my mind invents ridiculous ideas about what is making the noise.

Jesus describes the devil as a thief who wants to take what's ours and totally destroy us. We should be on our guard, listening and looking out for him. Rather like me when on a camping holiday, we shouldn't allow ourselves to rest too easily so that we won't spot the devil coming up to tempt us into going his way. Of course this doesn't mean we should obsess about this and constantly worry about what the devil is trying to do. But we should be wise and be aware that the devil is looking for an opportunity to strike and lead us away from God. This will particularly mean being aware of what can tempt us.

It can be easy to feel as if you are alone in facing temptation. But this passage reminds us that Jesus is our Good Shepherd. He is with us to help us resist temptation and He has put people around us who can pray for us and support us.

PRAY

Father God, thank You that we are not alone in facing temptation. Help us, wherever we are in the world, to follow Jesus' example and be on our guard so that we are able to stand firm against the devil's tempting. Amen.

READ:
JAMES 4:7–8

THURS 20 MAR

KEY VERSE
v7

'So humble yourselves before God. Resist the devil, and he will flee from you.'

I WAS RECENTLY reading some information that was apparently gathered from interviews with convicted rapists. Interestingly, but probably not surprisingly, most rapists said that they would give up fairly quickly if a woman put up a fight – they're generally looking for quick and easy gratification.

I once heard of someone who was approached by a mugger demanding he hand over his laptop. The victim shouted as loudly as he could, 'In the name of God, step away from me!' The mugger then turned and fled. Exactly why the criminal ran away is uncertain – was he worried about the noise his victim was making or did he fear God's judgment if he continued to rob this man?!

James tells us that, if we call upon God and resist the devil, the devil will flee from us. Yes, we will be tempted; that is inevitable. What is not inevitable is that we give in to this temptation. We have looked at a range of strategies that we can use to help us stand strong when we are being tempted and we have seen, through the example of Jesus, that it is possible to resist.

THINK

What might it mean for you to humble yourself before God? And how exactly could you resist the devil? How could these things help you to resist temptation?

FRI 21 MAR

READ:
MATTHEW 6:9–13

KEY VERSE
v13

'And don't let us yield to temptation, but rescue us from the evil one.'

WHEN I WAS a kid, I used to live near the local vets. My brother had a friend who sometimes came round to play after school. This friend had a dog. Whenever the boy's mother came to pick up my brother's friend, the dog would make every effort possible not to walk by the vets. He used to strain on the lead to try and cross the road. He was worried that his owner was taking him to the vets and he knew from experience that this was not somewhere he enjoyed going.

When we find ourselves being tempted, do we react in the same way as this dog, pulling away from it? Or do we blindly carry on, not thinking about where we might end up?

We already know that God is not the one who tempts us, but that He is with us to help us when we are facing temptation. Today's prayer will probably be a familiar one to you as it is the most famous prayer in the Christian faith – the Lord's Prayer. In teaching us to pray this prayer, Jesus wants us to recognise that we can rely on God when we face temptation. He will save us from the plans of the devil and He is our strength to help us stand firm against temptation.

CHALLENGE

What tempts you most strongly and frequently? Looking back over these studies on Temptation, what can you do to avoid and resist these temptations?

READ:
JAMES 1:2–18

KEY VERSE
V14

'Temptation comes from our own desires, which entice us and drag us away.'

PT2 APOLOGETICS

WELCOME BACK TO our musings on Apologetics: how we explain some of our beliefs about God. With brains fully engaged, let's continue. Perhaps the most important theological question of all is why a good God allows the people He creates and loves to suffer. First of all, it's important to acknowledge that really, we don't know the answer to that question. Ultimately, we'll only fully understand when we see God face to face.

CONTINUED»

CONTINUED

Having said that, there are a number of insights which can shed light on the problem of suffering. It's clear that our own choices make a difference to whether or not we and the people around us suffer. If I ate an entire 2 litre tub of ice cream, I would probably feel very sick. I would be suffering as a result of my own bad choice. If I force-fed someone else 2 litres of ice cream, they would feel very sick too. They would be suffering as a result of someone else's bad choice – mine.

All of us are tempted to make bad, selfish, lazy and impetuous decisions and these decisions have a profound effect on ourselves and other people. The temptation to make bad decisions comes not from God, but from within ourselves; from our own selfish desires. God loves us enough to let us choose how to act. The possibility for a good and godly choice is there, but so often we choose the bad and selfish option. This doesn't come close to explaining suffering completely, but it's a helpful start. And these verses from James also encourage us that if we are the ones suffering, that this pain can help to make our faith in God stronger (vv3-4). It's an opportunity for 'great joy' (v2)!

THINK

What examples of suffering can you think of? How many of these can be explained as the result of someone's bad choice? How might you explain the others?

READ: 1 PETER 5:8–11

KEY VERSE v8

'Watch out for your great enemy, the devil. He prowls around like a roaring lion, looking for someone to devour.'

THE BIBLE IS clear that the devil is a real being. He really exists, he really does hate us and he really does take any opportunity to harm us. He 'prowls around ... looking for someone to devour' (v8). We have to take our enemy seriously.

But these truths are the source of another difficult question. If God created everything and everyone and if God truly is good, why did He create the devil who is utterly evil? Frustratingly, there's very little in the Bible which explicitly deals with where the devil came from. Christian tradition teaches that Satan was once an angel, but that he rebelled against God, out of pride. (Jesus' words in Luke 10:18 reinforce this belief, as does one possible interpretation of Isaiah 14:12–17.)

It seems that God's gift of free will extends to His angels, too. Satan made the choice to turn against God and we may still suffer as a result of Satan's actions. However, we can look forward to the day when Satan will be totally destroyed. In fact, Jesus has already defeated him, through His death and resurrection. We can be certain that God, ultimately, has 'all power' (v11).

PRAY

Thank Jesus for defeating the devil. Ask for Jesus' help to notice what the devil is doing and to help you resist him.

TUES 25 MAR

READ:
PSALM 14:1–7

KEY VERSE
v3

'... all have turned away; all have become corrupt. No one does good, not a single one!'

WE NOW HAVE some idea of why we suffer and how and why the devil can harm us. But even if we can explain those things, why does evil exist in the world at all? Why has God even allowed the possibility that we might harm others? Why do those thoughts even cross our minds? Surely the world would be happier and more peaceful if there was no evil?

We've established that God won't force us to love Him since love that is forced isn't love at all (see 1/2 Feb). Perhaps, because of this, God has created a world in which love must be an active choice. For us to love God and act to please Him would mean nothing if there wasn't also the possibility to do what's evil. The existence of evil in the world means that goodness and love are deliberate choices. Our love for God becomes all the more meaningful if we choose to love Him even in circumstances when pleasing ourselves seems more attractive.

Ultimately, of course, we just don't know why evil exists! But surely what cures evil, not what causes it, is more important. We have God's promise that at the end of time, evil will be defeated and pain and death will be no more (Revelation 21:4).

THINK
Do some more research into the issue of suffering and work out what you think of it all. *The Problem of Pain* by C.S. Lewis is an excellent place to start.

READ: PROVERBS 16:33

KEY VERSE v33

'We may throw the dice, but the LORD determines how they fall.'

THERE'S A LOT in the universe which seems simply random. This can give us the impression that the world is cruel and arbitrary. However, this impression of the world comes from a misunderstanding of what randomness is. If something is unpredictable, it's not necessarily meaningless or without purpose. In fact, randomness can be highly purposeful. Unpredictable processes like genetic mutation and star formation were crucial to the origin and development of the universe, creating life, variety and beauty. God could work His purposes through these random processes, to create a huge, intricate and stunning universe.*

In biblical times, people used to make decisions by casting lots. They believed that God could speak and act through something that is seemingly random. There is certainly randomness in the universe, but we can be comfortable with this. While God is working out His purposes – even if we can't predict how – we'll find variety, new opportunities and new life.

CHALLENGE

Play a game of chance with some friends. Any card or dice game will do. As you play, talk about randomness; how God can work through it, and how random processes can produce life and beauty.

*Paraphrased from *Test of Faith: Spiritual Journeys with Scientists* ed. Ruth Bancewicz (Milton Keynes: Paternoster, 2009) p97.

THURS 27 MAR

READ: GENESIS 3:1–24

KEY VERSE v17

'… the ground is cursed because of you.'

ONE THING SCIENTISTS and theologians can definitely agree on is that the world is in a mess. Purely from an environmental point of view, climate change and natural disasters are ravaging our planet. So where is God in this? Why does He let earthquakes and volcanic eruptions happen? These are very complex questions. But these verses from Genesis give us a clue as to part of the answer. Some aspects of the earth's apparent fragility and unpredictability will always remain a mystery. However these verses suggest that part of the reason might be in man's rebellion against God (often called the Fall).

Just like the world around us, we're created by God. So when we sin by turning away from Him, we're alienated from the world, as well as from God. This profoundly damages us and our relationship with the world around us. Perhaps, as we see from this passage, the earth is damaged by humanity's ongoing rebellion in a very physical way. In any case, the more important question, regardless of our faith or our scientific expertise, is what part can we play in making the world better? Our actions can harm the world or heal it. And God's plan is to bring healing to the whole of creation.

PRAY

Father God, I'm so sorry for the times when my actions have harmed Your world. Please forgive me and help me to play my part in Your plan to heal it. Amen.

READ: LUKE 1:1–4

KEY VERSE
v3

'Having carefully investigated everything ... I also have decided to write a careful account for you ...'

HOW CAN WE be sure Jesus even existed? This is a vital question to ask. After all, if Jesus didn't exist, then following His teachings is pointless and claiming to know Him is nothing short of delusional. Luke would have had no doubt whatsoever that Jesus existed. He was surrounded by people who had known Jesus personally. But Luke wrote his gospel to set out exactly what Jesus had said and done. Luke was a doctor; a thorough, methodical man. He investigated Jesus' life very carefully and came to the conclusion that Jesus was exactly who He claimed to be.

It doesn't take much investigation to do away with the idea that Jesus never existed. Near enough all credible experts in ancient history (Christian or not) agree that Jesus was a real person.[1][2]

The challenge, then, is to go beyond this to consider whether Jesus really was the Son of God. So, if someone makes fun of you for believing in Jesus, challenge them to investigate Him for themselves.

THINK

How can you conduct a careful investigation of who Jesus is? How can you encourage your friends to do that?

---

1. Michael Grant, *Jesus: An Historian's Review of the Gospels* (New York: Simon and Schuster, 2004) p200.
2. Richard A. Burridge and Graham Gould, *Jesus Now and Then* (Grand Rapids: Eerdmans, 2004) p34.

WEEKEND

29/30 MAR

READ:

MATTHEW 28:1–15

KEY VERSE

v2

'... an angel of the Lord came down from heaven, rolled aside the stone, and sat on it.'

WHETHER WE LIKE it or not, Jesus' resurrection can sound a bit far-fetched. How many of us have ever seen a dead person come back to life? So it's entirely reasonable that non-Christians express doubt over whether the resurrection actually happened. So let's look at some of the alternatives. If Jesus didn't come back to life and leave the tomb, with an angel moving the stone away from the entrance, what happened?

Maybe the disciples stole Jesus' body, to convince people that Jesus had risen. Really, though? There were armed guards outside the tomb, to stop that very thing happening (see Matt. 27:62–66). And these guards would likely have been executed if they'd let the disciples get away with the body. Besides, all but two of the disciples (John died in exile, Judas hung himself) were later martyred for claiming that Jesus was the Son of God. Would they really have gone that far to defend something they knew was a hoax?

Or perhaps Mary and Mary Magdalene took the body. Honestly? The 'stone' in front of the tomb was a huge boulder. And when they later told the disciples that Jesus was alive, they didn't believe them anyway (Luke 24:11)!

And then there's the idea that Jesus merely 'fainted' on the cross, was buried, then woke up three days later and left the tomb on His own. Imagine a barely conscious man, starved for three days, trying to move a boulder and get past armed guards ...

There's no way! However unlikely it might seem, however far outside our own experience, the only reasonable explanation is that Jesus really did rise from the dead!

CHALLENGE

Don't just take my word for it! Look into theories about the resurrection for yourself. If you can get hold of a copy of *Who Moved the Stone?* by Frank Morison, it's well worth a read.

MON 31 MAR

READ:
1 CORINTHIANS 15:1–11

KEY VERSE
v6

'After that, he was seen by more than 500 of his followers at one time ...'

I HELP OUT with a youth club at my church on Wednesday nights. At one club night recently, one of our regular members walked through the door in a bad mood (which unfortunately is quite common for him). He decided to take out his bad mood on another guy standing by the door, pushing him over as he came in. This was totally out of order, so the club manager took the culprit to one side and gave him a talking to. But the guy flatly denied doing anything wrong! There were five or six people who had all seen the incident, but he claimed he'd never laid a finger on the other guy.

It's ridiculous to claim that something never happened when even a handful of people all saw it. Denying it happened when 500 people saw it is even more ridiculous! Writing to the Corinthian church, Paul points out that over 500 people saw Jesus alive at the same time, following His resurrection. In other words, Paul wants the Corinthians to know that Jesus' resurrection is an indisputable fact. He really did die and come back to life.

Today, we serve as 'witnesses' to Jesus' resurrection. We know the truth of it through the Bible, through our own faith and through having our lives changed by Jesus Himself.

PRAY

Lord Jesus, thank You for dying, rising to life and defeating sin and death. Please help me to trust You, follow You and love You. Amen.

READ:
1 CORINTHIANS 15:12–20

KEY VERSE
v17

'...if Christ has not been raised, then your faith is useless ...'

IF YOUR HOUSE was on fire, is there anything you'd run back through the flames to save? I'm tempted to say I'd save my bed, but I'm not sure how I'd do that ...

All of us own one or two things which are very precious to us and which we look after very carefully. I wonder if we could say the same about what we believe.

There are some questions in life which just aren't worth fighting over. In the end, it just doesn't matter whether we take communion sat in a circle or kneeling at the front of the church, or whether we worship using hymn books or swinging from the chandeliers.

But the fact of Jesus' resurrection really is worth fighting for with everything we have. The resurrection is the cornerstone of our faith. As Paul points out, if Jesus wasn't raised from the dead, then our whole faith is useless! There are some issues which we might let slide, or compromise on a little for the sake of unity within the Church. The resurrection isn't one of them. Jesus' bodily resurrection underpins our faith. It wasn't a mere 'spiritual' resurrection, Jesus certainly wasn't recovering from a faint, and the whole idea is not an elaborate hoax. Jesus died, rose again and ascended into heaven. Don't be tempted to compromise on those truths!

CHALLENGE

If someone asked you whether Jesus' resurrection really happened, what would you say?

WED 2 APR

READ:
JOHN 8:48–59

KEY VERSE
v58

'Jesus answered, "I tell you the truth, before Abraham was even born, I AM!"'

JESUS HAS ALWAYS fascinated people. Right from the beginning of His ministry, He has made people want to follow Him, to watch Him and listen to what He has to say. Even today, many people who would never think of themselves as Christians are fascinated with Jesus. This makes the task of evangelism much easier, but there is a problem connected with this: people will often stop short of accepting Jesus as the Son of God, claiming that He was a great teacher, but nothing more.

This conclusion is an appealing one. It lets us admire Jesus without accepting that He has any real authority to tell us how to live our lives. But this conclusion is impossible to accept if you look at what Jesus said about Himself. In today's reading from John, for example, Jesus is overtly claiming to be God. As C.S. Lewis famously observed, any person who says the things that Jesus said wouldn't be a moral teacher. They would have to be either mad (a bit like a person who thinks he's a poached egg) or be the Devil himself.

Jesus cannot be merely a great teacher. He is either a liar, a lunatic or the Lord. We must decide which of those three we believe Him to be.

PRAY
Lord Jesus, You truly are fascinating. Please help me understand more of who You really are. Amen.

READ: JOHN 15:18–27

KEY VERSES vv26-27

'But I will send you ... the Spirit of truth. He will ... testify all about me. And you must also testify about me ...'

I LOVE HISTORY documentaries. I especially love hearing about great ancient civilisations and some of the people who led them. A really skilful historian can almost seem to bring those people back to life, those who have been dead for thousands of years. But when the programme finishes, however interesting these people are, they're still dead. And really they are completely irrelevant to how I live my life today.

A similar accusation is often levelled against Christianity. Some say that what we believe is irrelevant; completely out of place in the twenty-first century world. After all, we're obsessed with a 2,000 year old book! But we're not just studying history. We're not following a leader who's been dead for 2,000 years. Jesus is alive and lives in us by the Holy Spirit. The Holy Spirit gives us Jesus' power to tell others about Him and change the world around us in His name. The Holy Spirit breathes life into the Bible, too, making it powerful, vibrant and challenging – far more than just words on a page. Jesus certainly isn't irrelevant. He's still changing the world today, through us. What we're fighting for *is* relevant and extremely important!

CHALLENGE

How is Jesus changing you? How is He acting through you to change the world?

FRI 4 APR

READ:
JOHN 14:5–14

KEY VERSE
v6

'... "I am the way, the truth, and the life. No one can come to the Father except through me."'

IF YOU TYPE the words, 'Why are Christians so' into Google, you're in for an unpleasant surprise! Nearly all of the words which appear to complete the question are highly negative. And one of the first words to appear is 'arrogant'. It seems that we Christians have got ourselves a bit of a bad press. In particular, people seem to think we're arrogant, which is quite hurtful!

In part, I suspect this reputation stems from some of the claims that Jesus has made about Himself. Today's key verse gives a particularly strong example. I sometimes wish I could agree with people who think of all religions as being equally valid ways to God. But Jesus doesn't leave that option open to us. He uses very exclusive language, describing Himself as THE way, truth and life and claiming that no one can come to God other than through Him.

However, we do need to be careful. Some Christians unfortunately think it's right to go around telling non-Christians that they're condemned to hell. It's unlikely that they'll save anyone this way! Sadly, they're just affirming the arrogant stereotype. So, let's not compromise on Jesus' status as the only way to God the Father, but let's also remember that our God is infinitely loving and accepting.

THINK
How can we insist that Jesus is the only way to God, while still loving and accepting people of other faiths?

READ:
ROMANS 4:18–21

KEY VERSE
V21

'He was fully convinced that God is able to do whatever he promises.'

HOPE PT2

WHEN HOPE IS mentioned in the Bible, it is often linked with a promise that God made to an individual or to a group of people. We see this very clearly in the story of Abraham found in Genesis, starting at chapter 12. God promised Abraham that he would be a father to a great nation, that his descendants would be more numerous than the grains of sand on a beach and the stars in the sky. What an incredible promise! However, when God made this promise to

CONTINUED▸▸

CONTINUED

Abraham, he didn't have children, was 75 years old, and his wife Sarah wasn't much younger!

As we look at that situation, everything within us would say that it just couldn't happen. Yet Abraham decided that he would take God at His word and put his hope in Him. One translation puts it like this: 'When everything was hopeless Abraham believed anyway, deciding to live not on the basis of what he saw he *couldn't* do but on what God said he *would* do' (*The Message*, 2002). That is Christian hope: making a decision that no matter how hopeless things seem, if God has promised us something, we will choose to believe Him and trust Him to bring it about. This applies to the promise of eternal life, which we've looked at previously, or a specific promise that God might have made to you in particular.

If you know the story of Abraham, you will know that God fulfilled His promise to Abraham. At the age of 100, 25 years after the promise was given, Abraham became the father of Isaac. God had kept His word, and proved Abraham wise when he chose to put his hope in God.

THINK

Have you ever believed a promise God has made to you, however unlikely it seemed? Or do you know someone for whom that's true? What can you learn from them?

READ:
1 PETER 5:1–7

KEY VERSE
v1

'I, too, am an elder and a witness to the sufferings of Christ. And I, too, will share in his glory when he is revealed to the whole world.'

TODAY'S PASSAGE MAY seem an odd one to include on the subject of hope but it's a passage that gives me great hope! This letter is written by Peter, who is now an old man and a respected elder in the church. He is writing to other church leaders asking them to lead well and to love the people in their care. This is the same Peter who as a young man and one of the 12 disciples continually put his foot in it, got things wrong in his enthusiasm and even denied knowing Jesus at a crucial moment.

But knowing God, and living lives with our hope firmly placed in Him, changes us. Peter is a real example of that. Through following Jesus and through the power of the Holy Spirit living in him, Peter changed and became the 'rock' on which the Church was built – as Jesus knew he would. For any of us who ever act without thinking things through, open our mouths without engaging our brains, or generally make a mess of things, there's real hope for us here. God can and does work in and through imperfect people just like us. Over the next few days we'll explore some of the different ways in which hope in God makes a difference in us and through us.

PRAY

Thank You Lord for all the people whose lives have been changed because their hope was in You. Please would You give me hope, and help me to see how You are changing me. Amen.

READ:
1 PETER 2:9–12

KEY VERSE
v10

'Once you had no identity as a people; now you are God's people. Once you received no mercy; now you have received God's mercy.'

WHEN PETER BEGINS this letter in chapter 1 he talks about how, as Christians, we are people who are living with 'great expectation' because of Jesus' death and resurrection (1:3). (We had a closer look at this on 18 Feb.) Right from the start of Peter's letter, he wants us to remember that we are people who live with hope, and living with hope should radically change how we live.

Peter goes on to describe what this hope looks like and in the part of the letter that we've read today, he reminds us that because of the hope we have we should see ourselves differently. In verse 10 the words, 'Once you had no identity as a people' remind us that we used to be a rabble, with no sense of order or direction. But now, as we are a people of hope that is no longer true – we do have direction and a sense of belonging. Peter describes how we are 'called out of darkness' and therefore are examples of light – the 'goodness of God' (2:9).

The hope and identity God gives us helps us to believe that what Peter writes is true – we are a chosen people, chosen by God to be His own.

CHALLENGE

Write out the names that Peter uses to describe the people of God in verse 9 and pin them somewhere you can see them. Each day remind yourself that as a person who is living with 'great expectation' these names are true of you.

READ: JEREMIAH 29:11–14

KEY VERSE v11

'For I know the plans I have for you ... plans for good and not for disaster, to give you a future and a hope.'

WHEN I WAS at school, I hated being asked, 'What do you want to do when you grow up?' The problem was I really didn't know. Part of me wanted to be a hairdresser but friends assured me that with my hair, no one would trust me to cut theirs! We can feel so much pressure to make good choices at school and college and end up feeling very anxious that we might be making the wrong decisions.

While it is really important to take good advice and to think things through, God doesn't want us to tie ourselves up in knots with fear about what the future might hold for us. Our view of the future should be different from people who don't share our hope. If you read the verses before today's reading (vv4–10) you will see that through Jeremiah, God tells His people to get on with life and make the best of living in exile. But above all He wants them to know that He knows them, and as they prayerfully seek God, He can be trusted with their futures and they can have hope because of this. He wants us to know this for ourselves, too. We can give our plans and choices over to God with the certainty that His plans are plans for good!

PRAY

If you are feeling anxious about the choices you are facing, talk to God about them and ask Him to give you peace and to help you trust Him for what lies ahead.

THURS 10 APR

READ:

MATTHEW 6:19–21

KEY VERSE

v21

'Wherever your treasure is, there the desires of your heart will also be.'

I WAS REALLY challenged a while ago by my seven-year-old niece. One night, her family's house was broken into and the burglar took a whole number of things, including the keys to their car and then the car itself. While the clean-up was going on afterwards, with the police going around checking for fingerprints and the insurance company wanting to know exactly what had been taken, my niece wondered out loud why the burglar hadn't just knocked on the door and asked if he could have the car. Her dad looked at her and asked what she meant. She responded, 'Well if he'd asked for it and said he needed it, we would have given it to him, wouldn't we?'

This really challenged me because I know if a burglar had knocked on my door and asked for my car, it wouldn't have occurred to me to say yes! But Maddie has grown up knowing that while having possessions is helpful, they are only things and we shouldn't put our hope in them. She has seen through the way her parents live that it's hoping in our treasure in heaven that really matters. And if you have that, then it's far easier to keep other things in perspective. Having hope in God changes what we value.

CHALLENGE

Make a list of all the things that you treasure most – both possessions and friendships. Go through the list and ask yourself honestly how important each thing really is.

READ:
1 TIMOTHY 6:3–16

KEY VERSE
v11

'But you, Timothy, are a man of God; so run from all these evil things. Pursue righteousness and a godly life ...'

WE'VE SEEN THIS week that having hope in God means that we experience a number of changes in our lives: it changes how we see ourselves, it changes how we view our future, it changes what we value, but it also changes how we behave.

The letters that Paul writes to Timothy are incredibly moving when you realise that Paul knows that the end of his life is near. He is taking this last opportunity to get down in writing all the things that he wants Timothy to know and remember as he continues in his life as a person of hope. At the end of this first letter, Paul tells Timothy that there will always be people who want to cause trouble, who will teach false things about life and God, and put material gain first in what they do. Paul closes by reminding Timothy who and *whose* he is. As he belongs to God and has put his hope in Him, he will therefore live a different kind of life. Paul wants Timothy to hold on to the hope of the eternal future that God has promised him, knowing that this will have an impact on how he lives his life daily. The challenge to us is to do the same – remember who and *whose* you are. This hope makes all the difference.

THINK

Do you have someone in your life who encourages you to hold on to your hope? Do you know of someone who may be in need of encouragement?

WEEKEND

12/13 APR

READ:

ACTS 1:1–11

KEY VERSE

v8

'... you will receive power when the Holy Spirit comes upon you. And you will be my witnesses, telling people about me everywhere ...'

THIS WEEK, MANY of us will be gearing up ready for Easter. But in this passage we've jumped ahead of Easter a bit – Jesus has died and risen again and has appeared to His disciples, amongst others. As the disciples are gathered together sharing a meal, Jesus sets out to tell them what is about to happen. Within the next few days they would see and experience even more remarkable things. They would see Jesus being taken up into heaven and they would experience the empowering of the Holy Spirit.

Jesus wants the disciples to know that even though He is no longer going to be with them physically, they still have a job to do. All that they have seen and learned was not to be kept to themselves, but to be shared with others. But Jesus knew they couldn't do this in their own strength – they would need the Holy Spirit. And so He tells the disciples to wait until the Holy Spirit came – and then they were to go right to the ends of the earth with His message of hope.

The hope Jesus gives us is not meant to be kept to ourselves. The gospel is a message of hope for us as individuals but God wants us to be people who will share that with others. After all, this hope is the greatest need of mankind! However, we, like the disciples, can't do this in our own strength. We too need the Holy Spirit to give us courage and boldness, to give us insight and to prompt us to share our hope with the people around us.

PRAY

Lord God, thank You that someone cared enough about me to share the good news of Your hope. Fill me with Your Holy Spirit so that I too can have boldness and courage, and a heart that wants others to know of the hope You bring. Amen.

MON 14 APR

READ: 1 PETER 3:13–16

KEY VERSE v15

'And if someone asks about your Christian hope, always be ready to explain it.'

WHEN WE READ the letters that are recorded for us in the Bible it's always important to remember that they were written by real people, to real people, in real situations. The people that Peter was writing to in this letter were threatened with persecution because of their faith – in fact this is what prompted Peter to write to them. Peter was writing to a group of people who were beginning to doubt whether they really had God's hope, because of the threats they were facing.

In writing to them, Peter aims to explain to them that God has not forgotten them, but he also challenges them on how they should live out their lives in the midst of suffering. For us, we may not suffer persecution but we will certainly experience peer pressure, so the message is the same: we are people of hope and that needs to be evident. Peter's encouragement is that people will see how we live, be struck by how hopeful we are and in time, find the source of our hope for themselves. Of course, if someone asks us about our faith in God and the hope we have because of Him, we shouldn't hesitate to tell them!

THINK

We may not face persecution but the challenge remains the same: do our lives stand out as being hopeful to people around us? If you were asked about why you have hope, how would you respond?

READ: PHILIPPIANS 2:12–16

KEY VERSE v15

'Live clean, innocent lives as children of God, shining like bright lights in a world full of crooked and perverse people.'

I HAVE A very vivid memory of a particular day when I was at college. Lectures had finished and a friend had offered to give me a lift home. As we drove she poured out her heart about a whole number of things that she was involved with, which she didn't know how to get out of. As we pulled up outside my house, she looked at me and said, 'There's no hope, is there?' I would love to be able to tell you that I shared with her that there is hope, that it can be found in knowing Jesus, and that I led her to the Lord there and then. But to my shame, that isn't what happened. I looked back at her and said, 'No, there doesn't seem to be' and got out of the car!

Many people feel like they're living in a dark place without any hope. They get up feeling hopeless and go to bed feeling hopeless. They feel the pull of many influences which would lead them into an even darker life. The interesting thing about light and darkness is that darkness can never snuff out light, but light can always banish darkness. When we hold out hope to another person, we are bringing God's light into their darkness.

PRAY

Often people really need someone to talk to about the things they are feeling hopeless about. Ask God to show you who those people might be. Pray for them now. Make an effort to listen to them and bring them God's light.

WED 16 APR

READ:
2 CORINTHIANS 5:11–21

KEY VERSE
v20

'So we are Christ's ambassadors; God is making his appeal through us. We speak for Christ when we plead, "Come back to God!"'

I HAVE TO admit, I've always thought being an ambassador would be a great job to have – to travel all over the world representing Britain, talking about a country I love with people who might not know how great a place it is.

In many ways we will all be ambassadors at some point. For example, I know a number of people who are real advocates for Apple products – always eager to talk about the latest creation and telling me what I'm missing out on. Their love for the brand is obvious and they fill me with hope of how owning this particular item will 'change my life'.

In 2 Corinthians, Paul tells us that as Christians we too are ambassadors, but not for a product; for Jesus. Jesus has called us to be people who share His word, His love and His hope with the people around us, because it has changed us so dramatically. But more than that, Jesus asks us to represent Him, to be His hands and feet and bring His light.

To represent God well, we need to know Him and His word. In order to share His promises, we need to know what those promises are. To grow in hope, it's vital that we know what the Bible says about the hope that we have.

CHALLENGE

Can you commit with a friend to get to know more of your Bible, and to share the promises that you find there? Start by finding and memorising five promises that God makes to us in the Bible.

READ:
EPHESIANS 1:19–23

THURS 17 APR

KEY VERSE
v19

'I also pray that you will understand the incredible greatness of God's power for us who believe him.'

I RECENTLY BOUGHT a bookcase and as I came to assemble it the instructions said it required two people to put it together. Being an independent kind of person, I decided that wasn't necessary and continued on my own. Very soon, I got into a bit of a mess and found myself trying to hold the bookcase together with both hands and both feet, completely unable to move to get the next piece in place. It all came crashing down around me. There I was surrounded by shelves, shouting at the instructions, 'I can't do this on my own!'

Often we try to live our Christian lives on our own. We try to be full of hope, kind to everyone and always ready to help, but we soon come to the point where we realise that we can't do this on our own. We need help from God and other people to live out our hope-filled life. And that's the way God intended it to be.

Paul wants the church in Ephesus to know that they don't have to go it alone – they have the Holy Spirit to help them. And the amazing thing is that exactly the same power that raised Jesus from the dead is at work in us. That is some power! If we are to be people who hold out God's hope to others, we need His power in us.

THINK

Why do you think it was so important for Paul to pray that his friends would understand the greatness of God's power?

FRI 18 APR

READ:
REVELATION 21:1–7

KEY VERSE
v4

'He will wipe every tear from their eyes, and there will be no more death or sorrow or crying or pain. All these things are gone forever.'

HOPE IS A wonderful thing. A lack of hope causes us great emotional pain, as the writer of Proverbs 13:12 tells us. We need to have hope in order to thrive in our daily lives. But as we've seen, the hope God gives us is not a wishful thinking kind of hope; crossing our fingers and hoping that everything will work out in the end. It's an absolutely certain hope placed in God, the creator and sustainer of the universe.

When we put our hope in God, knowing that He will take care of us now and in the future, we can be free from worry and free to love others and share our hope with them. This doesn't mean we won't experience difficulties and upsets every now and then, but we know that God has promised never to leave us, and that one day we will be free from sadness and trouble for ever.

As we come to an end of our studies on Christian hope, we see a beautiful picture of what God has promised to all those who love Him. Our hope in Him will be proved to be well founded. We can have certain hope in God, because He is the God who will always keep His promises.

CHALLENGE

In 2014, thousands of Christians will be getting together to share God's hope with others. Don't miss the chance to be a part of it! Check out www.hope-revolution.com for ideas, tips and details of what's already going on in your area.

WEEKEND 19/20 APR

READ:

1 CORINTHIANS 12:12–22

KEY VERSE V13

'Some of us are Jews, some are Gentiles, some are slaves, and some are free. But ... we all share the same Spirit.'

THE CHURCH PT3

HAPPY EASTER! AND welcome to part three of our look at 'The Church'. There is still a lot of prejudice in our world. People pride themselves on not being racist nowadays, yet all of us still hold some kind of prejudice. It might be to do with skin colour, a certain accent or just that we feel a person is different from us – not 'normal'. The international terrorist problems have led, in some cases, to more prejudice and have actually made us scared of some strangers in the street.

CONTINUED»

CONTINUED▶▶

God created the world to be a place where people could live in harmony together, but because of sin getting in the way it is hard to achieve that now. We can even see within the Church that there are distinctions between people in the way they worship, or the different churches they belong to. Yet, as our reading today says, we were all created by God and belong to the one Body, of which Jesus is the Head. We have the same Spirit within each of us and we are working and living for the same Jesus. He longs to see us living together peacefully, even though this will not be fully realised until He returns.

In this final section of our study on 'The Church', we will look at the diversity within the Church – the different people who are part of Jesus' Body. We will think about how we should respond to Christians who are different from us, and about how our differences can make the Church stronger. Although we're different, we can still live and worship God in harmony.

CHALLENGE

Try to identify some of the prejudices you may hold, whether towards Christians or non-Christians. Ask Jesus to work on your prejudices so that you can accept other people, value them and treat them with respect.

READ: PSALM 78:1–8

KEY VERSE v4

'... we will tell the next generation about the glorious deeds of the LORD ...'

I GREW UP in a church which included a lot of pensioners. At the time I didn't see them as particularly valuable, and I very rarely spent any time talking to them. I was far happier spending time with people of my own age. But a turning point came when I was 18. On the Sunday after I got my A-level results I walked into church and, straightaway, a lady in her seventies came over to talk to me. I'd never spoken to her before, but she asked me about my results, and explained that she'd been praying for me for years. This completely changed my impression of older people. I began to realise that although they might not be excitable and energetic, they have a lot of wisdom and a deep relationship with God. This woman had been making a real difference to my life by praying for me, even though I didn't know it. Perhaps someone is making a difference to your life in the same way.

The Church needs people of all generations to make it strong. It needs young people with energy, passion and idealism, but it also needs older people with wisdom, experience and a thoughtful, prayerful approach.

CHALLENGE

Make an effort to spend some time with an older person in your church. Be humble, listen to what they have to say and see what you can learn from them. How can you help them too?

TUES 22 APR

READ: GALATIANS 3:26–29

KEY VERSE
v28

'There is no longer ... male and female. For you are all one in Christ Jesus.'

I LOVE TO fix things. Whenever anything goes wrong, my first question is: 'How can I fix this?' There are times when this is helpful. When my kitchen sink got blocked, I rolled up my sleeves and spent the next hour or so pulling pipes apart, putting them back together and scooping out gunk. But I sometimes hit problems when my wife is upset about something. My instinct is to think, 'How can I fix this?' when often all she wants is for me to give her a hug and listen to her.

My female friends seem far more clued up on this. They seem to intuitively know when something needs to be done, or when someone just needs a hug and a listening ear. This is a small example of why men and women are equally important in the Church. The Church needs people who will get active and fix stuff, and it also needs people who can listen to others and empathise with them. Thankfully, sexism is becoming considerably less of a problem in our culture today. But perhaps we still feel a sense of a 'divide'. It is only through Jesus that we can be fully united. We can respect one another by recognising that we're equally valuable to the Church. We all have important roles to play, that are of equal importance.

THINK

Do you see members of the opposite sex as valuable? Do your words and actions show this? Do you need to make any changes here?

READ:
ACTS 10:34–43

KEY VERSE
v35

'In every nation [God] accepts those who fear him and do what is right.'

IF YOU LOOK at photos of Western missionaries in Africa taken early in the last century, you'll often see them surrounded by African people wearing the sorts of clothes you'd find in Victorian Britain! It looks very strange! These missionaries had kind of missed the point. For them, telling people in another culture about Jesus meant importing their own culture, as well as the Gospel. They thought that to worship God, you had to live and dress like an Englishman or woman.

But God isn't British! He loves and accepts people from all nations, and His Church is a global movement. Because God loves all nations, people from any nation are free to worship Him in whatever way fits their culture. We don't all need to dress the same way or pray and worship the same way in order to belong to the Church.

To 'fear' God is to obey Him, and so, as long as a nation's culture does not go completely against His ways, then no other nation can tell them they're wrong.

We should celebrate the cultural differences in the worldwide Church, and do whatever we can to serve and encourage Christians in other countries.

CHALLENGE

Have you ever seen the Church in a completely different culture? It's an eye-opening experience. See whether you can spend some time overseas, experiencing church in a different way and supporting the believers there.

THURS 24 APR

READ:
ACTS 2:42–47

KEY VERSE
v42

'All the believers devoted themselves to the apostles' teaching, and to fellowship, and to sharing in meals ... and to prayer.'

WHAT REALLY MATTERS in a church? What activities are vital and must always stay the same? Alternatively, what changes should we be open to making in order to ensure that our churches are relevant to our communities?

When we look at the early days of the Church, we see that they were committed to Bible teaching, prayer, worship, spending time together and helping the people around them. It seems fairly clear that a healthy church should still do all of these things today. But the Bible doesn't tell us exactly how the first Christians did these things, and it certainly doesn't say that we must do these things in the same way now. More and more churches today are exploring different ways of worshipping God and studying the Bible. Churches are worshipping with different styles of music, or even without music. Likewise, some preachers are looking at more creative and interactive ways of teaching God's Word. These new methods make sure that the really important elements of a church's life are still addressed, but in a lively, innovative way. As the Church, there are some things which we should always do, no matter what. But we should be open to new ways of worshipping God too.

PRAY

Pray for yourself and your church. Ask God for wisdom to understand what's really important, and for creativity to explore new ways of doing things.

READ: MATTHEW 18:15–20

KEY VERSE v20

'For where two or three gather together as my followers, I am there among them.'

A FEW YEARS ago, I was part of a prayer event in a football stadium. It was an amazing experience. Thousands of people were there, praying, singing and dancing together. The sight of it and the volume level was awesome – pretty overwhelming! Yet, on the other hand, I can also think of times when I've prayed with just two or three other people, and still had a profound experience of being in God's presence and hearing Him speak to us all, personally. It's tempting sometimes to assume that a church with more members must be better. However, this is far from what Jesus says. He tells us that our numbers aren't important. He is there when we meet in His name, even if there are only two or three of us. And when we meet in Jesus' name, His presence with us gives us power. He promises that our prayers will make a big difference.

You can probably think of a few huge churches. You can probably also think of a few smaller ones. Let's remember that bigger is not necessarily better. Whatever size your church is, God loves it – and He's there when you meet in His name. The size and power of our God is what matters.

PRAY

Lord Jesus, thank You for Your promise to be with us whenever we gather in Your name. Please help me to remember that You love my church, however many people we have.

WEEKEND

26/27 APR

READ:

1 CORINTHIANS 14:26–31, 39–40

KEY VERSE
v26

'When you come together, each of you has a hymn, or a word of instruction … so that the church may be built up.' (NIV)

ALL OF US have different skills, given to us by God. To build up the Church, we must all use the skills we've been given. Imagine a band whose members couldn't be bothered to play their instruments. It would be unlikely to sound good! The Church is similar. Each of us should play our part and use the talents or gifting we have. What if everyone in this band wanted to play the same instrument? It might sound OK, but it'd be nowhere near as good as if everyone played something different. Or, what if they thought their own, or the other musician's instrument, was more important?

God has given each of us different skills for a reason. If we were all the same, the Church would be seriously limited in what we could achieve. (It'd also be pretty boring!) We have different skills to support and complement each other, and to help the Church fulfil its mission of telling the world about Jesus. It works far better if we use what God has given us, rather than trying to be something we're not.

And, finally, what if the band all played at full volume, without listening to each other? It'd be chaos. It's important that we use our skills in a way that shows respect for the people around us. This is exactly what Paul is talking about in today's reading. If everyone in a church tries to use their God-given gifts at the same time, and without showing respect for other people in the church, it's just chaotic. Let's use our skills, but in an orderly way. Remember: it's about strengthening the Church – not about making ourselves look good.

THINK

What skills do you have? How can you use them in a way that strengthens the Church? Are you ever guilty of trying to be something you're not? Are you using your skills in a way that shows respect for others?

MON 28 APR

READ:
ACTS 6:1–7

KEY VERSE
v1

'The Greek-speaking believers complained ... saying that their widows were being discriminated against in the daily distribution of food.'

WHEN YOU LOOK around at your community, what do you see? What do people in your community need? Are there lots of homeless people, for example? Maybe there are lots of immigrants, who struggle to speak your language, or older people who are constantly stuck at home. The Church should not just declare but demonstrate Jesus' love to people around them. This means that we should be aware of what people in our community need and do what we can to meet those needs.

The apostles noticed a very simple need. There were widows in their community who weren't getting the food they needed. Something had to be done, so they appointed some people to take care of this. They clearly took this task seriously, too. The church leaders chose seven wise, respected and godly people, and laid hands on them to show that they were set apart for an important role. The Early Church took helping people seriously – and so should we!

THINK
What needs do you think people in your community have? How far does your church go to meet those needs? Think about what part you can play in helping your church meet the needs around you.

READ:
ACTS 15:1–6, 13–21

KEY VERSE
v2

'Paul and Barnabas disagreed with them, arguing vehemently.'

DISAGREEMENT CAN BE healthy! Within a church, there'll always be a variety of views; people should feel free to express those opinions. Some things are core truths of the Christian faith and are objectively true – nothing will change that. But on certain other topics there won't be a clear 'right answer'. In such discussions, the Church should be a safe place to talk, debate and share new ideas. This will help us gain a fuller understanding of who God is and what it means to follow Him.

This isn't to say that we should argue about everything though! The discussion in this passage from Acts gives us clues as to how we can share different ideas in a constructive way. Firstly, Paul and Barnabas involve the leaders of the Church in the discussion and make sure that both sides have the opportunity to put across their points of view. Together they check what the Bible has to say on the matter (vv16–18) and, above all, their goal is to build up the Church, not simply to win an argument! Because the Early Church dealt with this disagreement wisely, it brought a whole new dimension to the Church's life. If we handle our different opinions wisely too, it'll build up our own churches.

PRAY

Lord, please make my church a safe place to talk and discuss new ideas. Help us to handle disagreements well, so that we'll all know You better. Amen.

WED 30 APR

READ:
HEBREWS 11:32–12:3

KEY VERSE
v1

'Therefore, since we are surrounded by such a huge crowd of witnesses ... let us run with endurance the race God has set before us.'

THIS PASSAGE PRESENTS us with the image of an athletics stadium, crammed with supporters. Picture a group of marathon runners nearing the finish and straining for the line. You can almost hear the roar as the crowd cheer themselves hoarse, urging the runners on. The lesson for us is clear – keep going! As members of the Church, we're surrounded by people who encourage us, support us and spur us on. We're surrounded by heroes of the faith – people who've lived and followed Jesus before us. We're part of a family of believers stretching throughout time, as well as throughout nations. Let's learn from the people who've gone before us. Let's be inspired by heroes of the faith and let them spur us on to keep living for Jesus. When things get hard and running the race starts to hurt, hear the roar from the crowd of believers all around you shouting: 'Keep going!'

As members of the Church, we're all different in so many ways. But what we have in common is greater than our differences. We live for Jesus, and we're here to love Him, support each other, and make a difference in the world. These things transcend age, race, culture and even time. Let's keep spurring one another on.

CHALLENGE
Find out more about some heroes of the faith. Thank God for these people and think about what you can learn from them.

NOTES

NOTES

METTLE JANUARY–APRIL 2014

ORDER FORM

4 EASY WAYS TO ORDER:

1. For credit/debit card payment, call 01252 784710 (Mon–Fri, 9.30am – 5pm)
2. Visit our Online Store at www.cwr.org.uk/store
3. Send this form together with a cheque made payable to CWR to: CWR, Waverley Abbey House, Waverley Lane, Farnham, Surrey GU9 8EP
4. Visit a Christian bookshop

YOUR DETAILS	
Name:	
CWR ID No. (if known):	
Address:	
	Postcode:
Telephone No. (for queries):	
Email:	

SUBSCRIPTIONS (NON DIRECT DEBIT)	QTY	PRICE (INCLUDING P&P)			TOTAL
Mettle (1yr, 3 issues)*		**UK** £14.50	**Europe** £16.60	**Elsewhere** £18.75*	
(Subscription prices already include postage and packing)				**TOTAL B**	

Please circle which four-month issue you would like your subscription to commence from:

Jan–Apr **May–Aug** **Sep–Dec**

*Order direct from CWR or from your National Distributor. For a list of our National Distributors and contact details, visit www.cwr.org.uk/distributors

e-subscription and eBooks available. Visit **www.cwr.org.uk/mettle** for details.